TURGENEV

OTHER BIOGRAPHIES BY HENRI TROYAT

TURGENEV

HENRI TROYAT

TRANSLATED FROM THE FRENCH BY NANCY AMPHOUX

ALLISON & BUSBY

An Allison & Busby book
Published in 1991 by
W.H. Allen & Co. Plc
26 Grand Union Centre,
338 Ladbroke Grove,
London W10 5AH

Originally published in France under the title
Tourgueniev by Librairie Flammarion
First published in the United States by E. P. Dutton
Excerpts from *Tolstoy* by Henri Troyat translated by Nancy Amphoux.
Harmony Books edition, 1980, used for these excerpts.
Copyright © 1967 by Doubleday, a division of Bantam, Doubleday.
Dell Publishing Group, Inc. Reprinted by permission of the publisher.
First published in Great Britain by Allison & Busby, 1989

Copyright © 1985 by Flammarion
Translated copyright © 1988 by E. P. Dutton

Printed and bound in Great Britain by
Mackays of Chatham PLC, Chatham, Kent

ISBN 0 74900 076 7

CONTENTS

CONTENTS

Sixteen pages of illustrations follow page 88.

TURGENEV

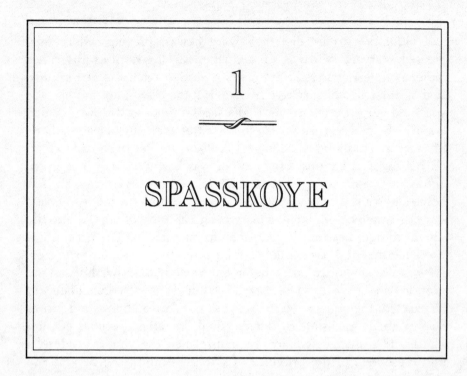

1

SPASSKOYE

Varvara Petrovna Turgenev, née Lutovinov, had an orderly mind. The child was hardly out of her womb before she called for her diary and inscribed therein, in a firm hand, "On Monday October 28th of the year 1818 my son Ivan was born at noon, in his house at Orel; he measured twelve vershoks." This was her second child. Nicholas, the first, had come two years earlier.* She was rather proud of these two male births, these promises of posterity for the name Turgenev, which was an old name from old nobility. The Turgenev clan descended from the Tatar khan Turga; beginning in the sixteenth century, Turgenevs had played an active part in the country's military and political affairs, as henchmen of the great Muscovite princes. There was even a martyr among them: Peter Turgenev, burned by Dmitri the Imposter for refusing to recognize him as tsar. By the eighteenth century, however, the glitter of their lineage had faded and its fortunes rapidly declined. But as the Turgenevs sank, the Lutovinovs rose—the family came originally from Lithuania and was undistinguished but rich. All its members were noted for their independence

*On November 4, 1816. The dates given here follow the Julian calendar which, in the nineteenth century, was twelve days behind the Gregorian calendar used elsewhere in Europe. Wherever two dates are given for the same event, the first refers to the Russian (Julian) calendar and the second to the Gregorian.

and peremptory manners; they were hawks, preying where they pleased. Varvara Petrovna's grandfather was a notorious miser; her father a hothead who led a punitive expedition against some peasants, in the course of which twelve of them lost their lives; her mother was widowed very young and married a second time—a widower named Somov who had two grown daughters. After enduring her stepfather's ill usage in childhood, sixteen-year-old Varvara Petrovna had to fend off his eager attentions. Her mother was hardly cold in her grave before her stepfather tried to rape her. To escape his clutches she left home and walked sixty versts* half naked through the snow to Spass-koye, an estate belonging to a maternal great-uncle of hers, where she sought refuge, begging her kinsman to take her in. The great-uncle was a hardhearted old codger, but he agreed to act as her protector. He was also an embattled bachelor and treated her so harshly that she grew to hate him with all her heart. For ten years, she complained and he exacted; they quarreled daily. After one last outburst, and just as he was about to disinherit her, he died, in rather peculiar circum-stances. His unexpected demise transformed the young Cinderella into the queen of the province of Orel: overnight she became the chatelaine of the vast estate of Spasskoye, which included twenty villages and more than five thousand peasant serfs, or *muzhiks.*

And this time she was determined to settle the score. She was twenty-six. True, her face was blemished by smallpox scars, her chin was too large and her nostrils too wide, but these shortcomings were offset by the glowing intensity of her gaze. Her tastes were somewhat masculine: she was fond of riding, rifle-shooting, and challenging the men to a game of billiards. She was a tyrant in the true Lutovinov tradition, intense and severe, but neighboring nobles courted her attentively all the same for her money. Among them she soon singled out a comely but impecunious officer named Sergey Nikolayevich Turgenev, six years her senior and a favorite with the women, whom he treated with courteous indifference. Her choice fell upon this appetizing morsel, and the morsel complied. How is a lowly junior officer, drowning in debt, his sole possession a village of one hundred and thirty souls, to resist the appeal of a plain but determined young woman who brings him a dowry of five thousand souls on a platter? Beneath his world-weary airs, Sergey was a heartless lover of luxury. On January 16, 1812, he married Varvara Petrovna and settled down to live with her in Orel. Five years later, having reached the rank of

*A verst is approximately two-thirds of a mile.

colonel, Sergey Turgenev retired from active duty and left Orel with his family to live on his wife's vast acres at Spasskoye-Lutovinovo, some ten versts from Mtsensk. A third son, Sergey, was born there, but he was partially paralyzed and died at sixteen.

At Spasskoye the retired colonel lived in opulence and idleness. As Sergey had no scruples about paying court to all the pretty women in Orel, and sleeping with the more easygoing serf girls on his estate, Varvara Petrovna spent her life in a state of furious jealousy and was constantly flying into rages. He sat them out, ironic and unmoved, and continued philandering as before. The truth of the matter was that the deceived spouse was too attached to her husband to be able to dominate him. She was so proud of her reputation as an ungovernable harridan that it infuriated her to find herself physically dependent upon a man, and she took her revenge for the humiliations she suffered at her husband's hands by maltreating the servants.

The domain over which she ruled as an absolute monarch included, in addition to the ordinary household staff, tutors and governors, singers, serf actors, and an orchestra. The household servants formed a brotherhood of some sixty families; they all lived within a few hundred yards of the main house, which had forty rooms. They worked as locksmiths, blacksmiths, carpenters, gardeners, cooks, land surveyors, tailors, shoemakers, upholsterers, coachmakers. It was like a little rural principality living in a closed economy. Everything needed for survival could be produced on the estate. Varvara Petrovna took great pride in the fact that she could sustain her little world without any outside help. She called her butler "court minister," and it was the "minister of the post" who brought her her letters from Mtsensk, after they had been scrutinized by the court minister, who decided, in light of their contents, whether the mistress of the house should be prepared for their perusal by a cheerful tune or a mournful one. Every morning at the same hour she sat in her office to hear the reports of her private secretary, estate manager, and steward, and, from her seat in a thronelike armchair on a raised platform, issued orders to her minions, who stammered with subservience. She had her own police force composed of retired guardsmen. Her justice was implacable. On her ruling, two serfs were sent to Siberia for failing to take off their hats in her presence. She had a waterfall rerouted because it disturbed her sleep. There were horsemen whose task it was to bring her a sort of porridge that could be made to her taste only in one village a long way from the house. Once, as a lesson to the inhabitants of Spasskoye who did not, in her view, show her

3

sufficient marks of respect, she even forbade the ringing of bells on Easter.

She was no less hard on her own family. Little Nicholas and little Ivan went in terror of their mother, who adored them but took sadistic delight in punishing them for trivialities. "I was whipped for some insignificant offense almost daily,"[1] Ivan Turgenev later wrote. She carried out her sentences herself. If the lad protested his innocence she would retort, "You know perfectly well why I'm thrashing you!" At one point Ivan was so disheartened that he tried to run away in the middle of the night and was prevented from doing so by his German tutor. The pressure of his mother's tyranny distorted his childhood. He felt himself constantly at fault in his dealings with this petticoated potentate; at the same time it gave him a secret thrill to be flattened by a woman. Unconsciously, he was already drawn to the ambiguous pleasure of yielding with hatred in his heart, and covering his fury with a compliant smile.

When he played with the serf children on the estate, however, there was nothing ambiguous about his self-assurance. Then he was the master. The little peasant boys, their congenital inferiority thoroughly drummed into them, never even attempted to return the blows he struck in the course of their horseplay. He explored the woods and fields with them, organized games of hide-and-seek, snared birds. By the age of seven he had already developed a sort of doting affection for birds. He could identify their songs at great distances and would crouch in the undergrowth for hours watching them flit from branch to branch. From birds, his lore broadened to include trees, ferns, and mosses. Reared in the countryside, his knowledge of nature was direct, firsthand, like that of the *muzhiks*. Most of them, however, were indifferent to the setting in which they lived and worked, whereas he never tired of wondering at the milky mist shrouding the pond, the birch woods with their trembling foliage, the old oak with its trunk split by lightning in which a couple of ravens sheltered. The smell of new-mown hay made him as dizzy as did the scent of perfume in the wake of a passing woman. He breathed the air of heartland, rustic Russia through every pore of his skin. By his own admission it was an old serf, Fyodor Lobanov, who taught him to love poetry. He later described this simple peasant and lover of beautiful words in a short story, "Punin and Baburin"; they would go off together and sit in the grass on the far side of the pond, where the old man would recite verses by Kheraskov and Lomonosov with high feeling and flourish. Fyodor Lobanov thought it a shame that the Turgenev children were being taught by German and Swiss tutors. He alone, he claimed, was defending the beauty of Russia against this cohort of intruders. "You are being separated from everything Russian," he would say with a sigh, "kowtowing to outside influences; you have turned to aliens for answers." Young Ivan, leaning against his shoulder, was exalted by his crude, fervent speech; and it was thanks to him and his father that Turgenev learned to read and write in Russian.

The library at Spasskoye contained vernacular editions of a few Russian classics. Ivan read them through eagerly, in secret. Kheraskov's *Rossiyada* (or *Russian Epic*) sent him into transports. It is true that although Varvara Petrovna was addicted to foreign culture, Sergey Nikolayevich—possibly for that very reason—wanted his sons to have a thorough grounding in their mother tongue. He urged them to practice writing in Russian and even suggested that they keep a diary, in which they should express themselves "in French on Monday, German on Tuesday, Russian on Wednesday, and so on by turns."

All his life Ivan thought of his remote, insensitive father and his cruel, despotic mother with a mixture of anguish and veneration. His parents were the cause of his penchant for women with strong personalities, of his horror of serfdom. "I was born and grew up in an atmosphere dominated by punches and pinches, blows, slaps etc"[2] he later wrote; and again, "I acquired my early loathing of slavery and serfdom by observing the shameful environment in which I lived."[3]

In 1827 the entire family moved to Moscow. Ivan and Nicholas, respectively nine and eleven years old, were enrolled initially in the Weidenhammer private boarding school; then, two years later, they were sent to the Armenian Institute, a secondary school run by an inspector named Krause. A few months after their admission there, Varvara Petrovna withdrew Ivan and had him continue his studies at home, while Nicholas was transferred to the St. Petersburg artillery academy. To furnish and embellish Ivan's mind, his mother called upon an assortment of tutors, including a poet named Klyuchnikov; their main task was to prepare him for university entrance examinations.

At fourteen, Ivan was a tall, slightly stooped boy with delicate features and a soft, gray-eyed gaze. He had a strong tendency to daydream and cared for nothing so much as reading. The Turgenevs knew Zhukovsky, whose poetry was universally beloved in Russia, and Zagoskin, the author of the famous historical novel *Uri Miloslavsky*. To Ivan these two men, whom he may have glimpsed in the drawing room at home, were godlike creatures dwelling among the clouds on Olympus. To keep abreast of Russian literary trends, he read two periodicals, the *Telescope* and the *Moscow Telegraph*. Even then, his artistic infatuations were mingled with amorous entanglements; his budding sensuality embraced poetry, nature, and women all at once.

Sexual pleasure was an early discovery. It happened one summer in the country. "I was only a stripling," he later told Edmond de Goncourt. "I was a virgin, with the kinds of desires one has at fifteen. There was a pretty chambermaid in my mother's house; she had a dumb-witted look about her, but you know, now and then one sees a face whose stupidity gives it a certain distinction. It was a wet day, soggy and rainy, one of those erotic days Daudet has just written about. Evening was starting to fall. I was walking in the garden. All of a sudden I saw this girl come straight up to me and take hold of me—I was her master, remember, and she was a slave—take hold of me by the hair on the back of my neck, and say, 'Come!' What followed was a sensation, like any other sensation; but that gentle tug on my hair, that one word, comes back to me sometimes, and the thought of it makes me so happy!"[4] On another occasion, at a dinner at Flaubert's, Turgenev told his friends, "My life is steeped in femininity. No book, no other thing, could have taken the place of women in my life. How can I put it? To me, love is the only thing that can produce a certain expansion, a fulfillment of the self that comes from no other source, don't you agree? For example, when I was a very young man I had a mistress, a miller's wife from the outskirts of St. Petersburg, whom I used to see when I went out hunting. She was charming, pale as dawn with a cast in one eye, which is quite common among our people. She would take nothing from me. Then one day she said to me, 'You must give me something.' 'What do you want?' 'Bring me some soap.' I brought her the soap. She took it and went away, then came back all blushing and said to me, holding out her perfumed hands, 'Kiss my hands like you kiss the hands of the ladies in the drawing rooms in St. Petersburg.' I threw myself at her feet. I can tell you, there has been no moment of my life more precious than that one."[5]

These glimmers of sexuality were to mark his adolescence less profoundly, however, than a platonic incident that took place before he had any sexual experience of women at all. The summer of his thirteenth year, he was vacationing at Nyeskuchnoye on the outskirts of Moscow. His parents' villa was next to that of the Princess Shakovskoy, and she had a nineteen-year-old daughter, Catherine, whose beauty, grace, and mischievousness left him dumbfounded. He fell blindly in love, and began paying a tremulous court to her, until the day he learned that she was his own father's mistress, that his father treated her like a dog, and that she was slavishly attached to him. Over thirty years later he based a short story on the episode, "First Love." He wrote, on the subject of his parents: "My mother was constantly anxious, jealous and ill-tempered, but not when my father was around. She was tremendously afraid of him, and he was severe and cold and remote . . . I have never seen a more phlegmatic or self-assured man, or one as authoritarian as he, or one as elegant withal." He wrote further, "I came to the conclusion that my father was totally uninterested in both myself and his family; what he cared for lay elsewhere, and he succeeded in making the most of it: 'Take everything you can get for yourself and let no one get the better of you; the only thing in life that really matters is to be your own master,' he told me one day."

Turgenev emerged doubly chastened from his sorry encounter with Catherine Shakovskoy: first, to find that the creature to whom he longed to devote his life did not care for him, and second, to learn that his more fortunate rival was none other than his own father. His response was not rebellion but resignation. It seemed perfectly natural to him that the young woman should choose a man as self-confident and distinguished as Sergey Nikolayevich in preference to himself. The heroine of "First Love," a mirror-image of Catherine, tells her suitor—a mirror-image of young Ivan—"No, I cannot love people I look down upon. I need someone who is strong enough, in himself, to make me yield to him." Ivan was not capable of making a woman "yield" to him. All he knew was how to adore on bended knee. So he choked back his tears and envied his father's firmness of purpose in matters of the heart. As for his mother, he felt sorry that she was so outrageously deceived, but it seemed obvious that a woman as headstrong and quarrelsome as she would not be able to keep anyone's allegiance. He himself was never so happy as when he was out of her sight.

Luckily, the next phase of his academic career placed him at a greater remove from the family. In 1833 he entered the philosophy department at Moscow University, and the following year his parents decided that he should transfer to St. Petersburg, which had a better reputation. He was delighted, because this meant, or so he thought, a permanent escape from his mother's overbearing influence. Also, it would bring him closer to his brother Nicholas, who was a cadet in the artillery academy in the capital. But he had hardly embarked upon his new student life when, on October 30, 1834, his father suddenly died, of complications from a kidney stone. Turgenev was affected, of course, but only moderately. He had admired his father for his confidence and success with women but had never felt any true meeting of minds between them. He was surprised to find how unmoved he actually was, beneath his impassioned exterior. Very early, he began to wonder whether he was capable of feeling any profound emotion about anything. He was exceedingly impressionable and readily swept away by enthusiasms, but a large and mysterious part of himself remained forever untouched, however demonstrative he might seem on the outside. For instance, he would take up some newcomer, become his firmest friend, charm him with affectionate speeches—all in perfect good faith—and, the next moment and in the same good faith, forget his very existence. For the present, what affected him most in his father's demise was the change it brought about in his own life. From then on, there was only his mother to keep watch over him and give him orders, and she was a long way away.

The first thing, he decided, was to become the perfect student. He attended every lecture and conscientiously crammed for exams, feeling quite at home in this atmosphere of studious fervor. He sat through the solemn lectures given by a handful of renowned professors in overcrowded amphitheaters, the stormy candlelit gatherings in low-ceilinged rooms, the endless rambling disquisitions on God, politics, and the future of the human race, the discussions of enthralling books and the hatching of dazzling projects in dense pipe smoke around the samovar. All his young fellow students imagined themselves to be revolutionaries; they abhorred serfdom; Hegel was their one true god. Turgenev followed the crowd. On the strength of his experience in the countryside he felt he could condemn slavery even more vehemently than his comrades. Whenever he spoke out against it as an institution that transformed *muzhiks* into cattle, he felt as if he were chipping away at his own maternal colossus.

These social preoccupations did not weaken his conviction that literature was his true vocation. Hearing that Gogol, the already-famous author of *Evenings on a Farm,* was to teach a course in general history at the university, he hurried to the lecture hall only to be bitterly disappointed: "He [Gogol] did not speak, but rather muttered indistinct and inaudible words, showed us little engravings of landscapes in Palestine and other Eastern lands, and seemed dreadfully confused," he wrote. "We were all convinced (and cannot have

8

been far wrong) that he understood absolutely nothing about history."[6]

A few weeks later he went to the opening night of Gogol's *The Inspector General* but failed to see what an extraordinary play it was. He talked literature for hours with his new friend Granovsky, he enthused, reviled, and dreamed of rivaling the greatest one day. By 1834 he had already composed a narrative poem entitled "Steno," in imitation of Byron's "Manfred." After hemming and hawing for a year, he finally submitted the manuscript, together with a few lesser efforts, to Pletnev, his professor of Russian literature, who was also a personal friend of Pushkin and Zhukovsky. Pletnev's stature was enhanced by the prestige of those two great names, no doubt, but he himself was a man of taste and goodwill. He read Turgenev's poem, considered it mediocre and childish, but encouraged the author to keep writing and even invited him to a literary soirée at his home.

Turgenev set out to attend this gathering of great minds in a quiver of admiration. His first encounter with real men of letters! In the entrance hall he was struck dumb: there, before his very eyes, stood Pushkin in person, taking leave of his hosts. Pletnev did not have time to introduce them. In a fur-lined coat, his hat already on his head, Pushkin called out, "Yes, yes, wonderful fellows, your ministers, there's no gainsaying that!" And swept out the door. Turgenev was never to forget that seamed face and those flint-sharp features. Still in a blissful trance, he entered the drawing room, where he met other authors of note, such as Voyekov, Grevenka, Odoevsky, and Koltzov. But his thoughts kept returning to that one lightning-swift glimpse of Pushkin. He was to see him again at a matinee concert a few days later. "He [Pushkin] stood by the door, leaning against the frame, his arms crossed on his broad chest, frowning discontentedly, his gaze darting here and there," Turgenev wrote. "I remember his small dark face, his African lips, the gleam of his large white teeth, his drooping whiskers, his dark, bilious eyes under his high forehead, almost without eyebrows, and his woolly hair. He glanced at me. The indiscreet attentiveness with which I was staring at him must have struck him unpleasantly. He shrugged—he looked to be in a bad mood, in fact—and moved away."[7] Shortly after this second near meeting, on January 27, 1837, Russia was staggered to learn that Pushkin had been killed in a duel with a Frenchman, Georges d'Anthès, who was paying court to his wife. This tragic death may well have hit Turgenev harder than that of his father. He joined the desolate crowds parading past the poet's corpse in an open coffin. Six weeks later came another loss: Turgenev's younger brother Sergey died.

Despite these blows, he passed his examinations and even submitted a few more poems to Nikitenko, another of his professors. "In transmitting to you my first feeble endeavors in the realm of Russian poetry," he wrote, "I would ask you not to imagine that I have the slightest desire to publish them. If I solicit your counsel it is solely in order to have your opinion of my writing, an opinion by which I set great store."[8]

He confessed that he had already translated parts of Shakespeare's *Othello* and *King Lear* and Byron's "Manfred." Nikitenko thought his student's efforts showed promise, and early in April 1838, thanks to him, the *Contemporary* published a poem called "Evening," written by Turgenev but unsigned. Reading his own verse in print in a famous review, Turgenev felt wings sprouting on his heels. Was it possible that he, an obscure student, a scion of the aristocracy still in his mother's thrall, could be about to soar aloft to the poets' paradise? Perpetually unsure of himself, he decided to set his sights lower and continue his studies, as Varvara Petrovna was commanding him to do. But to her, the learning dispensed at the universities of Russia was beneath contempt. Like everyone else of her class in Russia, she thought the true treasures of the mind were housed in Berlin. Much as it grieved her to be parted from him for so long, she felt her son ought to complete his education in Germany; and he, only too grateful for anything that would increase the distance between them, especially a frontier, was careful not to demur.

2

STUDY
AND ROMANCE

Sobbing and crossing herself abundantly, Varvara Petrovna accompanied her son to the pier on May 15, 1838. She had insisted that he go to Germany, and now she was sorry. In despair, she watched him board the *Nicholas I,* the ship that was to take him from St. Petersburg to Lübeck; he, meanwhile, could hardly wait to get under way. Until the very last minute his mother had bludgeoned him with threats, exhortations, and supplications. Once on the high seas, he felt delivered; at last he could stop being a compliant son and start to become a free man. He was twenty years old, his heart swelling with schemes. Facing the wind, he sniffed the tangy air and smiled as he listened to the water chuckling against the paddle wheels. In the first-class saloon sat a sprinkling of pretty, upper-class Russian women. The gentlemen were playing lansquenet. Despite his promise to his mother that he would never touch a playing card, Turgenev joined them. On May 18, just as he was in the midst of an unremorseful winning streak, a woman in disarray came rushing toward the table screaming, "The ship's on fire!" The passengers scrambled to the top deck in panic. "The chaos there was beyond description," Turgenev later wrote. "One felt that all these human beings, and myself more than the rest, were suddenly animated solely by the instinct of self-preservation. I recall that I clutched a sailor by the arm and swore that my mother would give him ten thousand rubles if he saved me."[1] He stared in dismay at the swirls of flickering smoke climbing up both sides of the smokestack and along the masts, and all he could think of was how to escape. He lost all self-control, piteously moaning "Too young to die!" and shoving aside women and children in his haste to be first into the lifeboat. Luckily they were within sight of the coast; the captain scuttled the burning ship offshore and the passengers were rowed to safety in longboats. The moment he felt solid earth beneath his feet, Turgenev became ashamed of his cowardice. His relief at having survived the catastrophe merged with his regret at having behaved so ignobly in front of so many people, all of whom would certainly carry every detail of the episode back to his mother. And so it was: His shipboard funk became the latest news item in Russian drawing rooms. Varvara Petrovna wrote indignantly, "How is it that the only thing everyone on board ship could hear was the sound of your lamentations? . . . Rumors come flying at me from every direction and many people have mentioned the incident, to my intense displeasure. 'Ce gros Monsieur Tourguéniev qui se lamentait tant, qui disait, "Mourir si jeune . . ." '* [That stout Mr. Turgenev, who kept wringing his hands, saying "To die so young . . ."] There were women aboard, mothers of children. Why do they all speak of no one but you? It is not your fault that you are a little stout, but to have been so frightened that other people could see it will leave a stain upon you—of ridicule, if not dishonor."[2]

Even at a distance his mother was still scolding him like a child. He was all the more eager to forget her by immersing himself in the life of the German university. In those days Berlin, which he had reached by road following his maritime mishap, was a middle-sized, peaceable, clean, dull town. The Germans rose at six in the morning, worked all day, and locked their doors by ten at night; the empty streets then sank into slumber, patrolled only by the indulgent eye of the beer-soaked night watchman. This center of industrious discipline was also a center of learning. At the university, Turgenev became an impassioned listener to lectures on Greek, Latin, history, and, above all, Hegelian philosophy. He immediately fell in with a group of young Russians in town, whose intellectual leader was named Stankevich. The focus of nearly every debate was Hegel's theories. Drawing inspiration from their deceased master, the students claimed that

*In French in the original.

the true subject of human history was the Absolute, that the world was proceeding logically toward a divine conclusion. In their eyes, this justified their resignation to an autocratic government. There were some, however, even in those days, who believed that a revolutionary lesson could be derived from Hegel's principles without distorting them. A movement of protest existed in the people; might this be no less justified than the order it sought to oppose? Turgenev, although in the very eye of this whirlwind of thought, did not take sides; he was to be mistrustful of extremes his whole life long.

Besides, he found that spiritual debate could be pleasantly reconciled with social divertissement. He attended balls, masquerades, the theater, rode horseback, and boasted of a successful liaison with a Mrs. Tyuchev, the mother of four. To keep an eye on him, Varvara Petrovna had sent a serf named Kudryashev to Berlin to act as Ivan's "secretary"; he was a mild, literate man, actually an illegitimate son of the fickle Sergey Nikolayevich. This bastard half-brother, only a year or two older than Turgenev, was devoted to him body and soul; but he was also obedient to his mistress and dutifully sent Varvara Petrovna a full account of Ivan's doings in Berlin by letter. Ivan also wrote his mother regularly. In his absence, her love for him was turning to obsession. In 1839 she wrote, in her diary, "John [Ivan] is my sun; he is all I see and when he is in eclipse I can no longer see at all, I don't know where I am." On another occasion: "Know that you are my star. I contemplate it, it guides me, I am waiting, waiting, waiting for you!" Pathologically possessive, she insisted that he tell her every intimate detail of his life. If his letters did not come often enough, she ordered Kudryashev to write and reassure her. When the silence went on too long, she threatened to take out her frustration on the servants: "I am indulgent enough, it seems to me. But if there are no letters from either of you in the next post I promise you I shall whip Nikolashka.* I don't like to do it, he's a very good, nice lad and I am not neglecting him, he is healthy and hardworking. But what can I do? The poor boy will just have to bear it . . . Take care you do not drive me to commit such an injustice."[3] Sometimes, to justify her epistolary blackmail, she blamed it on her own health, which she said was endangered by her son's indifference: "Write to me, or I shall no longer answer for my life, my sanity."[4] In the transports of her affection she tended to call him "my dear daughter, my Jeanette." "For

*One of Varvara Petrovna's young servants.

me," she wrote, "everything begins and ends with the two of you. You and your brother. I love you both passionately, but not in the same way. You are the one who hurts me most."

The son responded to this tempestuous fervor with hypocritical nonchalance. The more forcefully she displayed her masculine side, the more happily he indulged his feminine passiveness. She no longer spanked him, she only lashed him with her tongue; and he accepted her protestations of love and her remonstrances as he had accepted her hairbrush before. Upon learning that he had become Mrs. Tyuchev's lover, she rejoiced with male cynicism: "I told you before that you should read *Une femme de quarante ans* [*A Woman of Forty*]. That is my reply to your letter about Tyucheva. Please get the book and read it . . . I strongly wish you to have a woman like her, an old woman . . . Women like her are a treasure for a man. May it please God to keep you with her for a long time." But Mrs. Tyuchev suddenly died, and Turgenev consoled himself for her loss with less acceptable persons.

His womanizing and other undergraduate activities did not stop him from writing verse, which he then shut away in a drawer, not daring to show it to anybody. In St. Petersburg, meanwhile, the *Contemporary* published another of the poems he had left with Nikitenko, "On the Venus de Medici," signed ". . . v." But Russia was so far away, with its gilded cupolas, its birch forests, and its serfs, that he did not feel much affected by this minor personal triumph. Similarly, when a letter came from his mother informing him that the old house at Spasskoye had burned down, he felt only mildly put out. She implored him to come home, if only for a few days. Unwillingly, he went.

He was happy to see the country around Spasskoye again, with its misty ponds and shivering trees, the fields naked in the autumn chill, the humble old servants. A keen sportsman, he would set out at dawn with his rifle over his shoulder and come home late, cheerful and famished. His love of animals and almost pantheistic relationship with the natural world did not prevent him from shooting partridge and rabbits with wholehearted relish. This slaughter of the local wildlife even gave him a sense of a deeper, more primitive harmony with nature. On his return from his long rambles through the countryside, his spirits would fall at the thought of meeting his mother again inside the house, like some eternal governess. Now that her son was restored to her, she became more intransigent, demanding, and invasive than ever, and Turgenev, after his months of independence in Germany, found this daily appropriation of his person hard to endure. He told her so; she lost her temper. "If I had been in your place," Nicholas wrote to his brother, "I should not have come back to all the torments and weeping and tedium, I should have given thanks to God every day for the great blessing of living in freedom."[5]

Driven to distraction by Varvara Petrovna's scenes and vociferations, Turgenev left for St. Petersburg, without warning, on October 23, 1839. He spent some weeks there, ran the gamut of the literary salons, and met, *inter alia,* the poet Lermontov, first at a soirée given by Princess Shakovskoy and then at the New Year fancy dress ball of the Assembly of Nobility. "There was something malevolent and tragic in his physiognomy," he wrote. "His swarthy complexion and large, dark, staring eyes expressed passion, some hidden, evil force, a brooding contempt . . . His intimidating gaze contrasted strangely with the expression of his fleshy mouth, which was sweet, almost childlike."[6] He was too shy to introduce himself to the poet who, on the strength of the challenging, vengeful lines he had written on Pushkin's death, had become the *bête noire* of the authorities and the darling of the drawing rooms.

Thirsting for new horizons, Turgenev left Russia in mid-January 1840 and went to Italy by way of Vienna. He was dazzled by the grandeur of the ruins of Rome and the gaiety of its inhabitants. Stankevich, his friend from Berlin, was also there, seriously ill with tuberculosis. In the purity of his emotions and the courage with which he was preparing to die, this refined, unassuming, cultivated man seemed almost unreal to Turgenev. During the long walks they took through the town and countryside of Latium, they grew closer. The sight of so much beauty inspired Turgenev to take lessons in painting. In the evenings he liked to relax in the rooms of a hospitable Russian family named Khovrin. There, as was becoming habitual with him, he sighed soulfully after the mistress of the house, but without much hope. After touring Naples, Pompeii, and Genoa, he set out to return to Berlin, traveling by short stages and stopping off at Lago Maggiore, the St. Gotthard, Lucerne, Basel, Mannheim, Mainz, and Leipzig.

He had just reached Berlin, in July, when news came that Stankevich was dead. "A dreadful misfortune has struck," he wrote to his friend Granovsky. "I can hardly summon strength to tell you. We have lost a man we loved, in whom we believed, who was our pride and hope."[7]

A month later another friend came to occupy the place left empty in his heart by the one whose untimely death he was mourning. He met, and was instantly subjugated by, Michael Bakunin. He was a giant, voluble and florid, with a thick mane of light-brown hair and a piercing gaze, and he shared Stankevich's overweening passion for Hegel. The son of a rich landowner, he had rebelled, first against his father and then against the government. His sisters worshipped him to the exclusion of all else. For Turgenev too he became the only star in the firmament. Both were tall, impeccably groomed, and imposing, and they formed an inseparable duo: They sat side by side in the lecture hall, partied side by side in cafés, lived in the same house, read the same books, and held the same opinions in politics as in literature. But Bakunin was the lead horse, and Turgenev followed with a shade of hesitation. He admired the man as a force of nature but was afraid of being overpowered by him. Turgenev's own academic career was looking up: German philosophy had become an open book to him. He did well in his examinations, then returned to Russia and settled partly in Spasskoye, partly in Moscow.

At Spasskoye, the pleasures of shooting, daydreaming, and napping on an old leather sofa were soured by his mother's moods. She was growing increasingly fractious in dealing with her peasants and could not tolerate her son standing up for them, as he sometimes did. She ruled everything in her kingdom with an iron fist except a little girl of twelve named Varya,* whom she treated as a sort of adopted orphan but who was in fact her own illegitimate daughter. The father was Andrew Evstafyevich Behrs,† Varvara Petrovna's physician.

Turgenev played happily with little Varya, whom he treated like a younger sister, but his real interest lay elsewhere. An idle and indolent lordling himself, he had always been drawn to the common people, and had a confirmed weakness for serf girls, one of whom, Avdotya Ivanov, became his mistress. She was a fair-haired, gentle girl who worked as a seamstress for Varvara Petrovna and could hardly believe her good fortune when the young master's choice fell on her. However, when Varvara Petrovna learned of this ancillary liaison, she turned Avdotya away. Defying maternal wrath, Turgenev moved the young woman to a small apartment in Moscow where, in April 1842, she gave birth to his child, a girl baptized Pelagya. Turgenev, somewhat embarrassed, announced the circumstance to Varvara Petrovna and sought her indulgence for mother and babe. "How odd you are,"

*In the record books her name was given as Lutovinov; her married name was Jitova.
†Sonya Behrs, one of the doctor's daughters, was later to become the wife of Leo Tolstoy.

she wrote back. "I can see no wrong on either your side or hers. It's merely a physical passion."

Having thus been pardoned by the highest court, Turgenev turned his attentions to a different quarter: Tatyana, one of the four sisters of his friend Bakunin. He first met her at the Bakunin estate at Premukhino, where he was a guest. Tatyana was twenty-seven, deeply and widely read, and overflowing with fervor. She was a heavy consumer of the romantics, a great admirer of Novalis and Jean-Paul Richter, sensitive to the theories of Hegel and Fichte; life for her existed only in the seethings of ecstasy. Until that time her brother had been a sort of demigod to her, combining good looks, fierce energy, and knowledge. The attraction between them was ambiguous, both sensual and mystical; but with Turgenev's arrival Tatyana transferred her capacity for faith and admiration to him. He had such a noble air, with his height and regular features, dreamy eyes, and thick, light-brown hair. He dressed so elegantly—vests in subtle tones, tight trousers held down by straps under the heels, eyeglass dangling from a ribbon. And he was such a wonderful storyteller! Starry-eyed, Tatyana told herself that God had placed a genius in her path. He saw himself reflected in her eyes and had to admit that the image was not displeasing. True, she was no great beauty herself, with her long equine face and big mournful eyes. But who could resist the amorous appeal of her gaze? Their conversations became increasingly intimate. Suddenly the relationship that Turgenev had been cultivating frightened him. He had been diverted by sentimental badinage, now he was startled by the forest fire he seemed to have lit. Contemplating this fervid virgin, he was forced to admit that he was not really made for violent emotions. The proper atmosphere for him was one of cozy warmth, temperance, an artistic oscillation leading nowhere. About to be swept away in a hurricane, he scuttled back to safety. He tried to explain to Tatyana that, in the interest of his own peace and quiet, their relationship ought to be confined to the realm of ideology—this would make it all the more extraordinary. To her, this was a bitter disappointment. He sought to justify himself in writing: "We parted and have grown so foreign to one another that I don't know whether you will understand what prompts me to take pen in hand . . . Perhaps you imagine I am writing out of mere politeness . . . But I feel that I am not to be parted from you forever. I shall see you again, my good and wonderful sister . . . I have never loved any woman more than you, although I do not love you with a full and lasting love . . . You alone can understand me. For you alone I should like to be a poet, for you to whom my soul is bound so inexpressibly, so wonderfully . . . Oh, if only we could walk together one spring morning down a long avenue of lime trees, and I could hold your hand in mine and feel that our souls mingled and that all things futile, mediocre and evil had melted away forever!"[8]

These mellifluous protestations made it abundantly clear to the girl that he had tired of her. A few months later the relationship grew even more strained. Michael Bakunin had run deeply into debt to a German publisher in Berlin. Tatyana asked Turgenev to lend him a thousand rubles, to be repaid later out of her brother's share of their inheritance. The request discommoded Turgenev considerably, as he was short of cash himself at that point and didn't dare appeal to his mother. He eventually supplied the money, but only after a long delay, and he sent off a rather starchy letter accompanying the remittance. This offended Tatyana, who replied that she could not understand how he could speak to her in "such dry and scornful tones." He did not deign to answer. A lofty love was turning sour. Turgenev almost regretted having dedicated one of his poems to her—"Give me your hand and we'll go to the fields."

He was writing a great deal those days. Poetry was coming easily, and some of it was being published in the *Annals of the Fatherland* under the signature "T.L."[9]; he was also working on a one-act play called *The Temptation of St. Anthony.* In 1843 he published a narrative poem, "Parasha," again under the signature "T.L." This was an elegant, bittersweet piece, reminiscent of some of the work of Pushkin and Lermontov: the Russian countryside, a young woman oppressed by first love, a hero akin to Eugene Onegin, a "suitable" marriage, and "Satan sneering" at this triumph of the commonplace. There was nothing really new in it, but the author had an unmistakable gift as a storyteller, an eye for incisive detail, a harmonious, musical style. The influential critic Belinsky, whom Turgenev now knew personally, wrote a highly complimentary piece on "Parasha" in the *Annals of the Fatherland.* He particularly appreciated the author's "keen sense of observation, a profound thought springing from the inmost folds of Russian life, a graceful and acute sense of irony hiding a strong sensitivity."

Other writers treated his work with condescension, and some with contempt. But Belinsky's view prevailed, and Turgenev saw himself on the way to fame. Upon reading "Parasha," his mother wept tears of joy. "Contrary to all the critics," she wrote, "I find the tone quite perfect, as well as the ending which, your brother tells me, has been criticized. It's sweet, delicate, discreet . . . I agree with the qualities singled out for praise in the *Annals of the Fatherland*: it is all perfectly true and despite the critics I am proud that my son has ideas like this, new ideas . . . I have been brought some wild strawberries. We countryfolk are fond of tangible things. So now your 'Parasha,' your tale, your poem, smells of wild strawberries."[10]

Turgenev at the time was living in St. Petersburg with his brother, Nicholas, who was now an officer in a regiment there. Nicholas had broken off relations with their mother and set up housekeeping with a young German woman named Anna Schwarz, the daughter of a servant of Varvara Petrovna. The company of this rebel brother incited Ivan to greater independence and boldness. He passed his orals for his master of philosophy, did some work on a dissertation he was to submit for his final degree, and briefly contemplated a career as professor of philosophy at the university in Moscow; however, he soon gave up both the idea and the dissertation. In reality, he did not feel drawn to any "occupation." In his eyes, idleness and dilettantism were quite sufficient reasons for living. "You want to do nothing?" his mother wrote. "Then, bless you, do nothing! Live content wherever you like, however you like. Do you like to write, walk, shoot, travel? Who's stopping you? Spend the winter in St. Petersburg, enjoy yourself, go to the theater. In the spring come back to the country. In the summer we'll travel. In the autumn you can hunt and shoot. Live, and let us live with you." Elsewhere, "Go ahead and write, and God be with you; if you are successful you will continue and when you've had enough you'll stop. And that will be the end of it. Your true vocation is elsewhere. The homeland expects other things from you."[11] She considered that the best place for him to meet those expectations would be in the imperial administration. Obedient to her will, he unenthusiastically applied for a position in the Ministry of the Interior and was assigned to the offices of the ethnographer Dahl.

This purely honorary post left him more than enough time to write and enjoy himself. He dashed off a play, *Imprudence,* some lyrical verses that were published in the *Annals of the Fatherland,* and undertook to translate Goethe's *Faust.* At the same time, he was flitting through the drawing rooms and literary circles and going to the theater. In society, he tended to adopt the airs and appearance of a cynical, world-weary dandy. Romantic and negative, he irritated a few sour souls but charmed others, more sensitive to his fluent patter and gray-sea gaze. "It was universally agreed," Annenkov later wrote in his *Reminiscences,* "that he was incapable of a sincere word or feeling . . . His object was plain: to produce a literary effect upon his entourage and thereby gain a reputation as a character."

This ostensibly superficial and self-infatuated creature was nevertheless capable of strong emotions, his posing was merely the consequence of youth and inexperience. On October 28, 1843, at a shooting party, he met Louis Viardot, the husband of the soprano Pauline Viardot, to whose talent St. Petersburg was then paying lavish tribute. Shortly thereafter he saw the lady herself, singing the part of Rosine in the *Barber of Seville.* When on November 1 he was introduced to the singer he had just applauded, he immediately felt that his life had taken a decisive turn.

Pauline Viardot was twenty-two years old. She was not beautiful; her features were heavy, she had a wide mouth, protruding eyes, and stooped shoulders. But like some highly bred animal, she radiated a sort of majesty that utterly subjugated Turgenev. Struck dumb with admiration, he could hardly find words to compliment her on her singing. He wrote to her husband: "As for your wife—I shall not call her grandiose; in my eyes, she is simply the only soprano in the world."[12]

3

PAULINE VIARDOT

Daughter of the great Spanish tenor Manuel Garcia, sister of the celebrated soprano Malibran,* Pauline made her first public appearance in 1837, at the age of sixteen. In 1841, after singing in all the capital cities of western Europe, she married Louis Viardot, the director of the Opéra Italien in Paris, who was twenty years older than she. He was an urbane, cultivated, self-effacing man, content to play the thankless role of husband to a famous woman. She, meanwhile, flew from triumph to triumph. Her powerful, supple contralto voice had an extremely wide range and her gifts as tragedienne convinced the most exacting listeners. In St. Petersburg, where the Opéra Italien had just reopened, she was acclaimed as a goddess. Lines of university students pushed and jostled at the box office at dawn to get seats. Every aria was followed by an ovation, the audience stamped its feet and roared; when the performance was over flowers rained onto the stage. The fans of "the Incomparable" ran shouting alongside her carriage as she returned home from the theater.

Turgenev was admitted to his idol's inner circle and spent his evenings in the group of worshippers crowding her dressing room. Under the indulgent eye of Louis Viardot, he vied with the others in

*Who died in 1836.

proffering gallantries, snatching in midair every crumb that fell from the lips of the beloved who, with regal grace, permitted herself to be adored. She thought Turgenev a charming young man, to be respected more for his marksmanship than for his poetry. A huge white bearskin lay stretched on the dressing-room floor, with paws outflung and gilded claws. The right to sit on one of its paws, facing Pauline Viardot, was a treasured privilege. Turgenev was the proud occupant of paw number three; the remaining paws had been allocated to a general, a count, and a man named Gedeonov, the son of the director of the imperial theaters. Gedeonov was the singer's favorite, and presumably received some small concessions from her; but Turgenev did not despair of replacing him, one day, in the sentiments, and perhaps the arms, of his enchantress. He ruined himself in flowers and gifts.

It was the custom of this little court for each aspirant to tell a story during the intermission. Turgenev was unbeatable at this game. His improvised tales delighted Pauline Viardot, who listened to them half reclining on her divan. By dint of hard work and an ever-open purse, he gradually became the couple's most intimate friend. His passion for Pauline Viardot was accompanied by a fresh burst of literary activity. He published poem after poem in the *Annals of the Fatherland* and even submitted his first short story in prose, "Andrey Kolosov." Herzen met him and took a dim view. "A completely external personality," he said. "Boundlessly fatuous."[1] Belinsky, on the other hand, saw the young writer, still a shade too elegant, it was true, and a touch shallow and immature, as one of the nation's coming glories.

In those days the literati of Russia were divided into two camps: the Slavophiles, for whom there was no salvation, in art, philosophy, or even politics, except in traditional, Russian, Orthodox, grassroots sources; and the westerners, who maintained that all things good came from abroad. The former vibrated solely to the nation's past, its specific personality; they feared pollution from new ideas, they claimed that Russia should become the spiritual guide to all mankind. The latter proclaimed themselves open to the world, to progress; they wanted to see Russia merge with Europe. Turgenev, who had been a student in Berlin and was an admirer of Schiller, Goethe, George Sand, Hegel, and Fichte, felt drawn to the western school of thought; but his love for the Russian soil and people was such that he also understood the Slavophile attachment to any and every aspect of the nation's ancestral uniqueness. Whatever varnish of learning he may have acquired beyond its frontiers, he believed he belonged body and soul to the vast landscape in which the smallest blade of grass was an intimate friend. Why could not one love the West, admire its writers, painters, musicians, and philosophers, and at the same time be a kinsman of the illiterate *muzhiks* who prostrated themselves on the bare ground every Sunday in church? He was intensely aware of a dual allegiance, to Russia and to Europe; and so he refused to choose between Slavophile and westerner.

In art as in politics, he was wary of vehement opinions, peremptory stances, intellectual fanaticism. He always saw both sides of any proposition. He spent much of his time, however, in circles frequented by young people with more advanced ideas. He was a son of his time and so shared their liberal concepts. But there was no militant's soul beating in his breast. The meetings at which he was most at ease were at Belinsky's; when the critic moved to a suburban villa near St. Petersburg for the summer, Turgenev began paying him daily visits there. Belinsky, already suffering from tuberculosis, welcomed him with open arms and, between fits of coughing, his eyes bright with fever, launched into vehement discourses on God, the future of the human race, social injustice, and the latest literary trends. Vainly his wife begged him not to excite himself; dinnertime came, but Belinsky paid no heed. Turgenev was famished and betrayed his eagerness to repair to the table, whereupon Belinsky cried out, "Here we haven't even settled the question of the existence of God, and you think about eating!" Both men deplored Russia's backwardness, in comparison with other civilized countries. "What a wretched age!" Turgenev wrote. "When you look around, what do you see? Corruption is rife, serfdom is still with us, the barracks rise up like granite boulders in the foreground, justice is nonexistent, it is rumored that the universities are to be shut down, travel abroad is becoming impossible, there is no way one can have a good book sent to one, a black cloud hangs over anything pertaining to science and literature."[2]

And it was true that under the rigid rule of Nicholas I, the whole country was paralyzed, terrorized, too scared to move. It was as if time had stopped. People muttered and bowed their heads. Belinsky, meanwhile, was teaching his young friends that autocracy in politics was abhorrent and realism in literature a necessity. "If I were asked," he wrote, "what was the real merit of the new literary school, I should answer that the new school has turned away from the ideal of nature and human life, toward what is commonly called the crowd, has made the crowd its hero, is studying it with close attention and revealing it to itself."[3] Characters are no longer to be extraordinary, then, but ordinary, everyday people. Settings are no longer to be grandiose, but composed of details from everyday life; there are to be no more ecstatic dreams, only raw truth.

In his prose tale "Andrey Kolosov," Turgenev abandoned the Romantic idealism of his earliest works and produced a faithful picture of the student world he knew so well. From elegiac fantasies he moved effortlessly to social study, and Belinsky was grateful to him for this conversion to his own theories. "I have become somewhat closer to Turgenev," he wrote to Botkin. "He's an exceptionally intelligent, good man. Conversation and discussion with him are uplifting to the soul . . . He understands Russia. In all his judgments one can sense a character, and a sense of reality."[4]

It was probably Belinsky's influence that suddenly prompted Turgenev to resign from his civil servant's job in the Ministry of the Interior. He wanted no more files and schedules cluttering up his mind. Only with complete freedom of action, he thought, could he become a true creator. His mother despaired. After applauding his early successes, she now feared he was letting himself be drawn too far into Bohemia: "I cannot comprehend," she said, "your desire to become a writer! Is that an activity for a gentleman? To my mind, a writer and a scribe are all the same . . . Both scribble on paper for money . . . A gentleman should serve the state and forge a career and a name for himself in that service, instead of blackening paper."[5] As he persisted in his refusal to be a civil servant, she cut his monthly allowance. Some days, according to his friend Annenkov, he had hardly enough to buy himself a meal. He continued to attend every performance at which Pauline Viardot was singing, but he now sat in the top balcony. When the singer and her husband left St. Petersburg, he decided to follow them to Paris. On April 30, 1845, an indignant Varvara Petrovna wrote to a friend, "Ivan left here five days ago with some Italians; he plans to go abroad, with them or for them, I don't know which."

Turgenev was instantly captivated by the French landscape and the free and open ways of its inhabitants. The Viardots lived in the Château of Courtavenel, near Rosoy in Seine-et-Marne, thirty-five miles from Paris. Turgenev spent a few days there as their guest. What luck to sleep under the same roof as his beloved, breathe her scent in the rooms, hear her melodious voice from morning to night: It was all too good to be true. He became a close friend of her husband. Then, perhaps worried that he would wear out his welcome with both of them if he stayed any longer, he set off on a tour to the south of France and across to the Pyrenees.

He returned to St. Petersburg around mid-November 1845, but his thoughts kept straying back to the wonderful hours at Courtavenel. The greenery in the grounds, the sweet soft light of Île-de-France, the image of Pauline standing by the piano and singing in the evening for a few friends, all blurred together into a single wave of nostalgia. He wrote her constantly, telling her how deeply moved he was by his memories of his stay in the country and begging her not to forget him: "I read every article about you in the Prussian papers, you may be sure, and I was happy and well pleased with your triumph in *Norma* . . . Lord, how happy I should have been to hear you this winter!"[6] To take his mind off "the Incomparable," he was working hard, writing poems, translations, articles, and short stories. He also signed a contract with the *Contemporary,* under which he was to become a regular contributor to the review.

It was at about this time that he became acquainted with Dostoyevsky, whose first novel, *Poor Folk,* Belinsky had praised to the skies. Turgenev disliked the man, found him pretentious, awkward, and absurd. Dostoyevsky, on the other hand, was enthralled. "Turgenev is in love with me," he wrote to his brother. "What a man! I am not far from falling in love with him myself. A gifted poet, aristocrat, handsome, and rich, and intelligent, and cultivated . . . Nature has refused him nothing, I do believe."

Later, Turgenev and the poet Nekrassov collaborated on a spiteful epigram aimed at their vainglorious, gullible young colleague:

> *A harmless braggart, his features full of woes,*
> *Knight-errant Dostoyevsky by name,*
> *This new arrival is literature's shame,*
> *Like a swelling pimple upon its nose.*

Did Turgenev already guess that the author of *Poor Folk* was to become his archrival in the world of letters? To him, Dostoyevsky was a maniac; he represented everything Turgenev most abhorred in art: overstatement, heavy-handedness, lack of tact. He was delighted when, a short time later, Belinsky rejected Dostoyevsky's second novel, *The Double.* But these literary skirmishes provided only a momentary diversion from his *idée fixe:* to see Pauline Viardot again.

She was to sing in Berlin in January 1847. Posthaste, he went to Berlin. It made his mother wild to see him traipsing around at the heels of an "accursed gypsy." He had another excuse for the trip, however. Belinsky, too, was in Germany, where he had gone for treatment for his tuberculosis. His friends had taken up a collection so he could make the trip, and Turgenev gave him a room in the little apartment he rented in Berlin, and introduced him to the singer. Since Belinsky did not speak French and Pauline Viardot knew only three or four halting phrases of Russian, the meeting was a disappointment. But the sense of strain melted when the two men went to hear her sing *Les Huguenots* and again at a recital. Turgenev felt that she had surpassed herself. She had been "poignant" before, he said, but now she was "tragic." Annenkov, who had come to join the two friends, agreed. The three of them—Belinsky, Annenkov, and Turgenev—went on to Salzbrünn, where Belinsky was to have further treatment, and shared rooms there.

In the drowsy, peaceful spa Turgenev wrote "folk stories" at a leisurely pace, went for walks, and talked. Annenkov had already begun acting as his attentive memorialist and general factotum. An atmosphere of cheerful camaraderie prevailed in the little group; but suddenly Turgenev announced that he had to abandon his two friends. Leaving part of his baggage in their care, he set off for London, where Pauline Viardot was singing. Soon afterward he rejoined them in Paris, resumed possession of his belongings, and, in response to their queries as to the cause of his precipitate departure, blushed, shrugged, and said nothing. They had understood, however, that for him love outweighed friendship, and concluded that he was not to be counted upon. By this time Belinsky, who found himself no better for his stay in Germany, was being treated in a clinic in Paris. Turgenev went to visit him, but upon being told that the sick man was about to return to Russia, did not bother to say good-bye to him in person. From Courtavenel, where he had sought refuge once again, he wrote to his friend: "Dear Belinsky, so you're off to Russia. I cannot come to take my leave of you in person but I don't want to let you go without a word of farewell . . . I don't need to assure you that any and all good news from your end will bring joy to my heart. Although, as you say, I am a mere youth and on the whole a man of no consequence, I know enough to care for men of quality and I attach myself to them very durably."[7] Turgenev was never to see him again; Belinsky died the following year.

At Courtavenel, meanwhile, he sank voluptuously back into the French countryside, the good music, plentiful game, well-laden table, and Pauline Viardot. The château dated from the reign of François I and had a noble aspect with ash-gray walls, tall windows, steep-roofed turrets, and a moat. Formal flower borders spread out in front of the main façade; on the opposite side was an orangery. One's gaze wandered off to lose itself among banks of leaves.

Turgenev's room, its walls covered in "willow green," overlooked meadows and fields. The breeze brought him the scent of hay and lilacs. On his table stood a bouquet of wildflowers. What an ideal setting to write in! Oddly, this ultra-French province inspired him to produce ultra-Russian prose: At Courtavenel, he stared at France and dreamed of Russia. Every instant spent in the company of Pauline Viardot was engraved upon his memory. Walking in the fields with her, staring up at the star-strewn sky by her side, listening to her sing alone in the night, he responded to the magic of her presence as a happy slave. His worship extended to her gowns, ribbons, and slippers; she meanwhile treated him with regally smiling tolerance, and Louis Viardot pretended that nothing could be more natural than the amorous friendship between his wife and this charming Russian parasite.

At the beginning of October 1847 Pauline Viardot left for another tour of Germany. At once, the delights of Courtavenel palled and Turgenev removed himself to Paris, where he rented a room near the Palais Royal. He rose early, worked all morning and sent off story after story to the *Contemporary.* At two in the afternoon he paid a regular call upon Mrs. Garcia, Pauline's mother, whom he called "Maman." There he met "Maman's" brother, the jolly Sitchez, traded witticisms and went off for a ramble through Paris. He was especially fond of the Tuileries. "I watch crowds of children playing there," he wrote to Pauline Viardot, "all as lovable as cherubs, and so sweetly dressed. Their solemn childish caresses, little pink cheeks nipped by the first winter frosts, the placid, kindly air of their nannies, the beautiful red sun gleaming through the tall chestnut trees, the statues, still water, majestic dark gray walls of the Tuileries: I find it all infinitely pleasing, it rests and refreshes me after a morning of work."[8]

After this meditative promenade he returned to the Palais Royal, pausing in a café to read the gazettes; then off to Le Véfour restaurant for a frugal repast, and then, at top speed, to the theater. He was to be seen at the Variétés, the Opéra-Comique, the Opéra. Afterward, in his long letters to Pauline, he would comment upon the productions he had applauded. He also advised her, tactfully and intelligently, about her own career. His opinions were those of a connoisseur. Informed of the singer's every word and deed by the newspapers, he gloried in her successes and moaned because he was not there to hear her in *Norma* or *Romeo*. Learning that she was to sing Iphigenia, he urged her to read Goethe, to deepen her understanding of the rôle.

Trying to unite himself ever more closely with this Viardot family that had now become his own, he began to learn Spanish. Soon he could read Calderón in the original, and found him magnificent. But he was also keenly interested in French literature. Michelet's *Histoire de la Révolution française* was a peerless masterpiece, he said, and he also thought highly of George Sand's latest novel, *François le Champi*— "simple, true, poignant." "It is plain to see," he wrote, "that she [Sand] has had enough of socialists and communists, is exasperated by them and is now plunging with delight into the fountain of youth of naïve folk art."[9]

In the meantime, the circle of his Russian friends in Paris had widened. He was seeing quite a lot of Herzen, Ogarev, Annenkov, and a family named Tuchkov, recently arrived from Rome, in which there was a daughter who was secretly infatuated with him. "He was so tall as to be almost a giant, and broad-shouldered too," wrote one of his contemporaries, the Slavophile publicist Leontyev. "His dark gray eyes were deep and thoughtful. In those days his hair was thick and dark and, if I remember aright, rather curly but with a touch of gray. He had a most winning smile. His hands were large and beautiful, a man's hands. He was then about thirty."[10]

Turgenev tended to be rather capricious with the women in this little Parisian clique, bright one day and gloomy the next, now babbling, now bleakly taciturn. Sometimes he would put on fancy dress and perform stunts to divert people. His fickleness of temper and his clowning eventually got on Miss Tuchkov's nerves, and after sighing for him she turned away in disdain. For Turgenev, playing the fool was a brief respite from the underlying misery of his existence: his prolonged separation from Pauline Viardot. Thus far, he saw no one who could take her place in his heart.

Bakunin, meanwhile, who had unexpectedly returned to Paris, and Herzen were all in a twitter over the political events taking place in the capital. They sniffed the first mutterings of revolution in the air. "The world is in travail," Turgenev wrote to Pauline Viardot. "Many people are working to abort the birth. We shall see."[11] As usual, he refrained from strongly partisan sentiments. He read the papers to find out what was going on, he approved of the "reformists" who were organizing banquets to protest against the monarchy of Louis-

Philippe, he criticized the "fanatical and counterrevolutionary" speech made by Mr. de Montalembert in the Chamber of Peers but, unlike Herzen and Bakunin, he did not long for a general cataclysm that would stand the country on its head. He was in Brussels for a few days when Louis-Philippe abdicated. At six in the morning of January 26, 1848, the door of his hotel room was flung open and somebody bawled, "France has become a republic!" "Unable to believe my ears," he wrote. "I leaped out of bed and rushed from the room. A boy was running down the corridor opening all the doors left and right and hurling his stupefying exclamation into every room. Half an hour later I was dressed and my bags packed, and I returned to Paris by train the same day."[12] At the frontier, the rails had been unbolted from the cross-ties and the passengers had to go on by coach to Douai, where the railway was in operation again. Everybody was very excited; most people said they had high hopes of a more just future. He heard only one old man sighing, "All is lost, all is lost!"

In Paris, Turgenev stepped off the train into the whirl and fever of the street. Red, white, and blue flags were waving everywhere. The provisional government seemed unable to control the agitation of the crowds. Political clubs were springing up like weeds. There was a banking crisis, a violent workers' demonstration against the Day of the "Fur Hats" (the national guard), a stormy mass meeting outside the Constituent Assembly. Bakunin, amid all this confusion, was in transports of joy. At last he was in his element: the convulsion of the oppressed masses. He was living in a barracks with some armed laborers and preaching bloody revolution. His hotheadedness worried Turgenev, who began, prudently, to put some distance between them. In April 1848 Bakunin left for Germany, to prepare for an uprising of the proletariat of Dresden. He was arrested and thrown into prison.

In Paris, the revolution was going around in circles, rudderless; time was being wasted in bickering and talk. Turgenev, profoundly unconcerned by all these ideological explosions, would escape from the city now and then and take a walk through the surrounding countryside, dreaming of his inaccessible Pauline. "I spent more than four hours in the woods, sad, distraught, attentive, absorbed and absorbing," he wrote her. "The impression nature makes upon humans is curious. At the bottom there is a cool bitterness, as in all the smells of the fields, and a touch of serene melancholy, as in birdsong . . . I am bound to the soil! I am happier contemplating the nervous thrusts of the wet, webbed foot of a duck scratching the back of its neck on the edge of a pond into which it has waddled up to its knees, than all the things the cherubs (those illustrious flying faces) can see in the heavens."[13] In Paris, his bucolic calm was shattered by a fresh surge of public discontent. The provisional government was replaced by an executive commission; the national workshops set up for the unemployed proved ruinously expensive and unproductive; the Constituent Assembly ordered their closure. The directionless mobs threatened to take up arms. It was clear that a fratricidal confrontation was about to pit the forces of law and order against the desperate workers. On May 15, 1848, Turgenev watched the quelling of a workers' demonstration on behalf of Polish independence. "What struck me was the way the cocoa and cigar-vendors moved through the crowds," he noted. "Greedy-eyed, happy and indifferent, they looked like fishermen hauling in a well-filled net."[14]

On June 23 he went out to walk the boulevards, where the resistance was said to be gathering steam. Near the porte Saint Denis he found a barricade, guarded by laborers in work clothes and surmounted by a red flag. He was standing on the sidewalk observing the scene with curiosity and detachment, when the military charged in serried ranks and the first shots were fired. He fled in panic down the rue de l'Echequier.

In the heat wave of the ensuing days, he stayed shut up in his room, sweating and trembling. This whole affair was no concern of his. For once being Russian was a stroke of luck. From time to time he heard muffled detonations. The rebels were being shot in the district town halls. The revolution had been quelled. General Cavaignac was to be president of the Council. "What surprised me most was how utterly impossible it was for me to ascertain the people's feelings at a time like this," Turgenev wrote to Pauline Viardot. "I swear to you, I simply could not make out what they wanted, what they feared, whether they were revolutionary or reactionary or simply longing for peace and quiet. They looked as though they were waiting for the storm to blow over."[15] Great as his detachment was, he could not help feeling appalled by the violence of the reprisals, summary executions, and mass arrests. "The reactionary side is quite intoxicated by their victory and will now show themselves in all their cynicism,"[16] he wrote a little later.

Herzen, whose extremist views had aroused suspicion, found it expedient to leave Paris for a while. Turgenev had nothing to fear: he was neutral. From this brief experience of revolution he learned only one thing: a horror of chaos, lies, useless sacrifice, and systematic massacre. He was a man of reason and peace, who longed for a better life for the people, but without upheavals. More than ever after this exposure to tumult and bloodshed, he felt himself destined for contemplation, love, and writing. Where could he go to escape the rigors of life? There was only one safe place: Courtavenel!

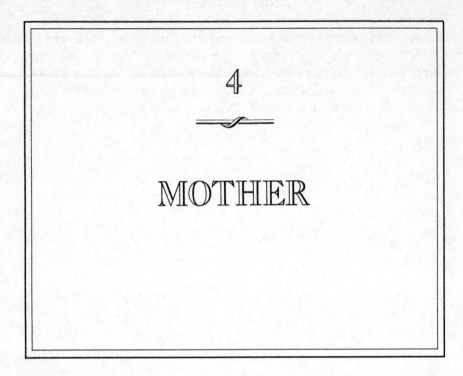

4

MOTHER

Toward the end of June 1848, Turgenev and Pauline Viardot met again at Courtavenel; she was back from a triumphant tour and resting with her family. After a long period of relations restricted to correspondence, he could not get enough of the woman herself, of her ebony hair smoothed over her ears, her ardent eyes, her broad mouth made for singing and loving. She was deeply touched by the amorous perseverance of her Russian giant with the strong features and weak character. It was probably at this point that she finally gave herself to him, but in doing so she was not yielding to blind passion; rather she was rewarding, in her way, a long and faithful friendship. He knew this, but was so enraptured that he was prepared to be content with a charitable approximation. Any crumb dropped from the divine table was worth snapping up. The husband pretended not to notice. Only Pauline Viardot's seven-year-old daughter Louise took offense at her mother's affection for the intruder. He now spent a few weeks of perfect happiness with a woman who, after an interminable pursuit, had deigned to share herself with him, in secret, now and then. When he left her that autumn to travel through the south of France, the tone of his letters was very different. In the past he had written with respectful admiration, now he dared to speak openly of his love:

"Good morning, most loved, best and dearest woman, good morning, unique being . . . Beloved angel! . . . The only, the most loved, God bless you a thousandfold! . . . Greetings from the heart to your treasured self."[1] The image of this beloved went with him every step of the way on a long voyage that took him, by stagecoach and train, to Lyons, Valence, Avignon, Nîmes, Arles, Marseilles, Toulon, and Hyères.

While he was amusing himself discovering France, his mother was begging him to come back to Russia. On March 14, 1848, Tsar Nicholas I, preoccupied by the possible repercussions elsewhere in Europe of the political upheavals in Paris, issued a manifesto calling upon "all loyal citizens to combat the French revolution." This was a pressing invitation to any Russians residing in that diabolical country to return to their native land. But Turgenev stubbornly continued to hang on there. It was too much! Having already pared his allowance to the bone, Varvara Petrovna now angrily withdrew her financial support altogether. When he got back to Paris at the beginning of November he found himself genuinely penniless and was forced to ask Krayevsky, the director of the *Annals of the Fatherland,* for an advance, in return for which he agreed to become a regular contributor to the review. He was also still writing for the *Contemporary.*

Short stories, poems, comedies—his productions were many and varied, and already highly esteemed in the far-off country to which he refused to return. In "Petushkov" he analyzed the damage wrought by passion upon a man chained to an inaccessible woman; the story was undoubtedly inspired by his own experience as a humiliated suitor of Pauline Viardot. Others—the majority—such as "Khor and Kalynch," "Bezhin Lea," "Meeting," "Kasyan from the Beautiful Lands," "The Country Doctor," "The Werewolf," "Lebedyan," and "Strawberry Water," were reminiscences of his sportsman's rambles through the Russian countryside. They portrayed simple, true characters: rough *muzhiks,* children afraid of the night, hard-hearted lords, scheming stewards, the whole little world of the provinces. In all of them, the anxious churning and toiling of humans shrank before the tranquil majesty of nature. The beauty and indifference of trees, fields, and sky overpowered all lesser creatures; and the disproportion between them generated a feeling of affectionate compassion for mortals of every condition. Here the peasants appeared not as beasts of burden with crippled brains but as complex beings, intimate with the round of the seasons, suffering from their landlords' brutality. In this way the author suggested all the horrors of serfdom without any heavy underlining. He had no thesis, made no indictment; he only gave an accurate, calm portrait of reality.

The censors, misled by the moderation of these descriptions of rural life, let the stories pass with occasional minor changes. Each story is a complete picture in itself. Every detail contributes to the overall impression, and the melancholy that radiates from the unadorned, bitter tales is intensified by their artistic perfection. Readers were clamoring for more, so Turgenev was now spending many hours at his desk. He had rented an apartment at 1, rue Tronchet; but the following spring an epidemic of cholera broke out in Paris. One night, feeling sick and vomiting, Turgenev thought he had caught it. Herzen, who was living in the same house, had him carried to his own rooms and nursed him assiduously despite the danger of contagion, an act of devotion all the more meritorious as his friendship with Turgenev had cooled considerably since the 1848 uprising. The patient seems to have been needlessly alarmed, however, because he was soon on his feet again and, fleeing the big city and its cadavers and malodorous miasmas, took shelter once more at Courtavenel.

Unfortunately, he did not find Pauline Viardot there—she was in London—and had to content himself with Uncle Sitchez and his wife. He divided his time at Courtavenel among writing, walking with Sultan the dog, fishing, and playing billiards. The Sitchezes soon returned to Paris, however, and Turgenev, alone in the huge silent house, felt the full weight of his solitude. There was one interlude: a visit from Gounod, who went to Courtavenel to work on his opera *Sappho*. "Gounod spent the whole day walking in the Blondureau woods in search of an idea," Turgenev wrote to Pauline Viardot. "But inspiration, fickle as any woman, did not come and he found nothing. He will seek his revenge tomorrow."[2]

After Gounod left, the only people he had to talk to were the gardener and an old serving woman named Véronique, who cooked for him. He was fond of loitering in the kitchen yard among the chickens and would play with Sultan, feed the rabbits, and supervise the cleaning of the moats, and then, in the evening, be overcome by nameless apprehensions. Sitting in the drawing room playing solitaire, he suddenly thought he heard two deep sighs close to his ear. "It gave me a mild case of gooseflesh," he wrote to Pauline Viardot. "Crossing the hall, I wondered what I should have done if I had felt a hand suddenly grasp mine, and was forced to admit to myself that I should have screamed like an eagle. One is distinctly less brave by night than

by day. I should like to know if the blind are afraid of ghosts."
Another time, going out into the courtyard, he observed, with fear
and wonderment, the secret murmurs of the night: "The sound of
blood in one's ears, and breathing. The brushing, the constant whisper
of leaves. The cry of cicadas; there were four of them in the trees in
the courtyard. Some fish came up to make a little sound like a kiss at
the surface of the water. Now and then a drop fell, making a little
silvery sound, or a twig broke; who broke it?"[3] And above all, the
dark abyss of the sky with its myriads of stars: "The thousands of
worlds hurled in profusion into the farthest depths of space are nothing other than the infinite expansion of life, of this life that fills every
place, penetrates everything, needlessly and for no purpose causes a
whole world of plants and insects to be born and seethe in a drop of
water."[4]

In the course of these nocturnal meditations he felt both a boundless admiration for the beauty of the sky and a dread of the supernatural forces governing the universe. His sleep was often agitated. Pauline Viardot would appear to him in nightmares in some ominous
guise. Sometimes, too, he dreamed he was a bird*: "I go to blow my
nose and find a long beak in the middle of my face . . . Then I rose
into the wind uttering a great cry of triumph, and then dived down
to the sea, beating the air in bursts as gulls do. I was a bird at that
moment, I promise you, but now, as I write this to you, my recollec-
tions of my sensations as a bird are no more distinct than those of
yesterday's dinner . . . You are going to laugh at me and you will be
right."[5]

Pauline Viardot was so much in his mind that he sometimes
worried about her husband losing patience with his insistent presence
at Courtavenel. "For what reason is Viardot displeased?" he wrote to
Pauline. "Perhaps he does not like my staying on here?" He finally
dared to address her in the intimate form, but in German: "Beloved,
may God keep thee and bless thee."[6] From time to time he went to
Paris, but only to read the English newspapers containing stories
about her. He would have liked to go more often but was still short
of money; at Courtavenel he lived off the Viardot family. He was a
little embarrassed about this, but hospitality to friends in need was a
law among Russians, and besides, he was convinced that one day soon
he would be able to repay his hosts a hundredfold. "By the way, it
may surprise you that I was able to make the trip to Paris, in view of

*He was to remember this dream when he wrote his short story "Phantoms."

the state of my finances," he wrote to Pauline. "But Mrs. Sitchez left me thirty francs when she went, twenty-six of which have now gone. In fact, I am living here as in an enchanted castle; what more does a single man want? I hope that this dearth of money will soon cease and that somebody back there will finally begin to wonder, 'What can he be living on?' "[7]

But "somebody"—that is, Varvara Petrovna—"back there" was continuing to play deaf. He appealed again to Krayevsky for a thousand-ruble advance, and promised to inundate him with copy in return. Faithful to his word, in early 1850 he sent off "The Diary of a Superfluous Man" to the *Annals of the Fatherland;* while Nekrasov received, for the *Contemporary,* a comedy entitled *The Student,* which later became *A Month in the Country.* But the money was no sooner in his pocket than it flew out again in every direction. There were so many debts to pay! Turgenev appealed to Krayevsky once more, but this time could get only two hundred rubles. It made him furious to have to beg for subsistence, while back in Russia his mother was reigning like an Oriental despot over thousands of serfs. Perhaps there was no alternative, after all, but to go home again. No, no, not yet! "Russia will wait," he wrote to Pauline Viardot, "that huge, dark face, immobile, veiled like the sphinx of Oedipus. She will swallow me in due course. I seem to see her heavy, inert gaze fixed upon me with brooding attention, as befits eyes of stone. Rest easy, Sphinx, I shall come back to you and you will be able to devour me at your leisure if I fail to solve your riddle! But leave me in peace just a little longer! I shall return to your steppes!"[8]

Suddenly, a bombshell: the indestructible Varvara Petrovna was seriously ill. She wanted her son at her bedside and sent six thousand rubles to pay his debts and traveling expenses.

At this, he felt morally obliged to go. In despair, he bade farewell to Pauline Viardot, who was not heartbroken to see him depart. She was quite thankful for his love, but looked upon him as a voluble, overgrown child, fickle and moony, who could in no way deflect the deeper current of her woman's life. She, though possessed of a keen sense of the theatrical when on stage, had a horror of dramas in everyday life. Everything should be simple, she believed, between people of good company. Louis Viardot himself was not greatly troubled by minor trespasses against conjugal fidelity. He was sincerely fond of the gifted parasite, who might or might not be Pauline's lover. By tacit agreement, the couple avoided quarrels and respected appearances. Face was saved on all sides. They could all three, after all, be fond of one another.

As he was packing his bags, Turgenev wrote to Louis Viardot: "I take with me the most affectionate memory of you; I have learned to appreciate the excellence and nobility of your character and, believe me, I shall not feel genuinely happy until I am able once again to roam the beloved meadows of Brie by your side, gun in hand . . . The fatherland has some rights, no doubt; but isn't one's only true fatherland there where one has found most affection, where the heart and mind feel most at home? There is no spot on earth I love as well as Courtavenel . . . In me, my dear Viardot, you have a devoted friend who will never fail you."9

Varvara Petrovna was deeply disappointed in her sons. Nicholas, the eldest, had resigned his commission in the army, become infatuated with a woman who was less than nobody, and was living from hand to mouth; Ivan, the younger, spent his time writing, traveling abroad, and flailing about in the wake of "a circus performer." Both of them were escaping her authority. She wanted them under her thumb, complete with wives and grandchildren. In her domineering mania she had ordered a wooden panel to be posted at the entrance to the estate, reading "They shall return."

Turgenev rejoined his mother and brother in Moscow. Varvara Petrovna was better, and at first seemed happy to have her sons beside her. They took advantage of this to ask her for a regular income, that they might live decently. She pretended to sympathize, and offered each a piece of property. But when it came to making the gift official she changed her mind, and actually ordered the stewards to sell off the year's harvest overnight, together with all the reserves in the barns, so that there was no seed left for the next year's crop. Both brothers refused this offering, which was no better than an empty box, and one that she could take back at any moment, moreover, since the document had not been notarized. Turgenev exclaimed indignantly, "You torment everyone who breathes free air around you! You can't understand that we are no longer infants, that for us your behavior is an offense. You're afraid to give us anything for fear of losing your power over us. We have always been respectful sons, but you have never trusted us. The truth is that you don't trust anybody or anything. All you trust is your own power. And what has it given you, your power? The right to make everyone's life a misery." Panting, her eyes starting out of her head, Varvara Petrovna moaned, "Am I such a monster?" "No," Turgenev answered, "you aren't a monster, I don't know myself what you are or what goes on inside you . . . Who is happy in your presence? . . . Everybody is afraid of you, but we might have loved you!" Pale with anger, Varvara Petrovna pronounced dully, "I have no more children. Leave!"[10] and left the room herself. The next day Turgenev tried to see his mother again. She would not let him in and, picking up his portrait, broke it and threw it to the floor. When a serving woman hastened to pick up the fragments of shattered glass, she ordered her not to touch them; the debris lay where it had fallen for four months.

Evicted by their mother, Ivan and Nicholas withdrew to the little farm of Turgenyevo, which came to them from their father, while she, sick with fury, moved back to Spasskoye. A scant eighteen versts separated her from her sons, but she had decided to ignore them. She forbade them her door and did not answer their letters. From time to time Turgenev would go to inquire after her health. Young Varya, Varvara Petrovna's illegitimate daughter, would see him coming in his hunting outfit, booted and muddy, gun in hand, cartridge belt around his waist and game bag at his side, uneasy, timid, skulking, his features drawn by the fatigue of the long trek. In a quick sentence or two she would tell him what mood his mother was in that day and off he would go, head down.

These days, he had another subject of concern: his daughter Pelagya (now known as Pauline or Paulinette). When he first went abroad he had left her with Varvara Petrovna, who treated her harshly, like a servant. Could he do nothing more for this child of eight, this reminder of a youthful transgression? She was the very image of her father. The village people poked fun at her, calling her "mademoiselle" or "the bastard." In his distress, Turgenev appealed to his guardian angel, Pauline Viardot, and she, with a generosity bordering on irresponsibility, agreed to take the child in and bring it up in her own family. "With regard to little Pauline," he wrote, " you already know that I have decided to follow your orders and am concerned only how best to carry them out quickly and well. I shall write to you from Moscow and St. Petersburg daily, telling you everything I arrange for her. I have a duty to perform and since you are good enough to interest yourself in the matter, I perform it gladly. If *Dios quiere,* she will soon be in Paris."[11] A few days later he took it upon himself to inform his correspondent of the child's origins: "I shall tell you in two words about my affair with the girl's mother. I was young—it was nine years ago—and, bored in the country, I noticed a rather comely seamstress whom my mother had taken into her service. I said a few words to her, somebody came to see me, I paid, I left, and that was all . . . Thereafter, the person turned out as best she could and you know the rest. The most I can do for her is to better her material circumstances—that is an obligation, and I shall fulfill it—, but it would be impossible for me even to see her again. You are an angel in your every word and thought but, I repeat, all I can do for her is to protect her from want. And that's what I shall do. The child will have to forget her mother ever existed."[12]

Delighted with the arrangement proposed by Pauline Viardot, Turgenev took his daughter to St. Petersburg and sent her from there on October 23, 1850, carefully chaperoned, to Paris. And imagined thereby that the little Russian peasant girl would be transformed into a perfect French young lady. He himself had no plans to return to France for the time being. He could not be away from Russia any long period of time, there was too much that needed his attention there. His brother, Nicholas, was so hard up that in a moment of self-abnegation Turgenev ceded his share of the Turgenyevo estate to him. He was still hoping his mother would have second thoughts, find herself more charitably disposed, and agree to help her sons by signing over part of the income from her estates to them. For the time being, however, Varvara Petrovna was proving very stubborn. She was suffering from dropsy and went to Moscow for treatment. Bedridden, hardly able to breathe, she felt her end approaching and began to wonder whether she had not made a mistake somewhere in the conduct of her life. One evening, overcome with remorse, she seized a scrap of paper and wrote, in French, "My children! Forgive me. And you, Lord, forgive me too; for pride, a mortal sin, was always my besetting sin." Nicholas came running. She blessed him with shaking hand and called for her other son. But Ivan was in St. Petersburg. By the time he was located and could get to Moscow, she was dead.*

The grief Turgenev felt at the loss of his mother was mixed with a tenacious resentment of her feudal, vain, cruel, and obstinate personality. "My mother died without seeing to anything," he wrote to Pauline Viardot shortly after the funeral. "She left this great swarm of lives, all dependent upon her, out in the cold—and I do mean cold. Now we shall have to do what she ought to have done. Her last days were most wretched. God preserve us from such a death! She spent all her strength trying to avoid the truth. On the eve of her death,

*Varvara Petrovna died on November 16, 1850.

when the rattle had already begun, she had an orchestra playing polkas in the next room. But we owe only respect and pity to the dead and so I shall say no more. And yet, as it is impossible for me not to tell you everything I feel and know, I shall add just one word, and that is that at the end of her life, I am ashamed to say that all my mother could think of was how to ruin my brother and me. The last letter she wrote to her steward contained exact and definite orders to sell everything for a pittance, burn the crops if need be, so that nothing . . . Well, one has to forget and I shall do it with all my heart, now that you know, you who are my confessor. And yet I feel that it would have been so easy for her to be loved and mourned by all! Ah, yes, God preserve us from such a death as hers!" In the same letter he expressed his delight at "Paulinette's" arrival in France and the good account of her sent by Pauline Viardot: "I do hope this great change will save her. Kiss her for me, please. Now that I have more money than before I will not hesitate to spend as much as a thousand francs a year [on the child's keep]. Set her to learn the piano. I shall send you money in ten days or so. I am very happy to think that you see a resemblance between us and that it pleases you. Send me a little pencil drawing of her, one of yours. I repeat that I shall come to be quite attached to her in the end, if I know you are fond of her."[13]

A little while later, sorting through his mother's papers, Turgenev came upon a sort of personal diary, scribbled in pencil.* The contents appalled him. "What a woman!" he wrote to Pauline Viardot. "What a woman! I did not close my eyes all night. God forgive her everything. But what a life! I promise you, I am still in a daze. Oh, yes, let us be true and good, if only in order not to die like that."[14]

The brothers divided their inheritance without dispute. Spasskoye fell to Turgenev's lot. Overnight, he was a rich man, thanks to a mother whose memory he abhorred. Having become a landowner, he authorized a few serfs to purchase their freedom but did not carry out any wholesale emancipations. Although he disapproved of serfdom, he was afraid that once the *muzhiks* were on their own, landless and without capital, they would be even more wretched than they were under his benevolent rule. Besides, such a step would have been very much the exception in those days, and contrary to his temperament. He was a man of dreams, afraid of action. Any serious decision was like a precipice yawning at his feet; it frightened him.

Well heeled now, he divided his time between St. Petersburg and

*Varvara Petrovna's diary has not survived.

Moscow, giving dinner parties, showing himself in drawing rooms, and savoring the success of his early stories. His comedies, amiable Russian *marivaudages,* also pleased the public. He wrote that on the opening night of his play *A Provincial Lady* his heart beat strangely. "Just as the curtain rose I spoke your name in a whisper," he told Pauline Viardot. "It brought me luck." At the end, the audience applauded wildly. "I was expecting anything but a success like that," he wrote. "Can you believe that I was called back, and with such vociferations that I ran away, quite beside myself, as if a thousand demons were after me . . . I am very sorry now that I ran away, because people might think I was putting on airs."[15]

Alongside his theatrical achievements, Turgenev continued to polish his little provincial tales. He was thinking of bringing them out in one volume, entitled *Memoirs of a Sportsman.* * But would the censor's office, which had authorized publication of the single stories, approve them once they were assembled into one book presenting a picture of Russia that was, on the whole, dark and pessimistic? To smooth the way, Turgenev consulted a man named Ketcher, a translator of Shakespeare and friend of the late Belinsky, and of Stankevich and Herzen. He wanted to dedicate the volume to Pauline Viardot: "You have not yet answered my request in regard to the dedication. I hope you will not refuse me this happiness, especially as, for the public, there will be only a row of stars in place of your name."[16]

While sighing after Pauline Viardot with one eye, the other contracted a weakness, in the spring of 1851, for a pretty serf girl named Theoctista Petrovna Volkov, who belonged to some Turgenev cousins of his; he bought her from them for a very steep price, freed her, and made her his mistress. This liaison, contracted for purely physical reasons, left his mind free to dream of the other one, the diva, the one to whom he wrote, in one rapture, "I kiss your feet for hours at a time. A thousand thanks for your adorable nails."[17]

Another play of his, *Where the Cloth Is Thin It Will Tear,* was soon to be produced. On October 1851 Shchepkin, the actor, took him to make a ceremonial call on Gogol, for whom Turgenev felt a filial admiration. He found the author of *Dead Souls,* standing at his tall writing table, quill in hand. Dressed in a short overcoat, green velvet vest, and brown trousers, Gogol seemed terribly tired and old. "A long, pointed nose gave his features a cunning, foxlike air," he wrote. "Soft, swollen lips beneath a close-trimmed moustache added to the

*There have been many titles in English, such as *A Sportsman's Notebook. Sketches from a Sportsman's Album.* etc.—T.N.

disagreeable impression. Their indefinite contour seemed to me to express the negative side of his personality. When he spoke they parted to reveal decayed teeth. His small chin was buried in a broad black velvet cravat . . . Looking at him one was unavoidably led to think, 'What an intelligent, strange, unhealthy creature.' "[18] On this occasion Gogol, who was ordinarily rather taciturn, waxed eloquent. He discoursed on art and literature, said he was delighted with his visitor's little stories. Seated next to him on a divan, Turgenev drank in his words. But when Gogol tried to tout the merits of censorship, he quickly moved to change the subject; behind the immensely gifted creator of *Dead Souls* and *The Inspector General*, he encountered the blinkered, dyed-in-the-wool reactionary that Gogol, under the pressure of his entourage, had lately become. Not long after, Turgenev saw him again at a public reading of *The Inspector General*. Then, on February 24, 1852, at a meeting of the Benevolent Society, he learned from Panayev, his colleague on the *Contemporary*, that this singular author was dead. Shocked, he wrote to Pauline Viardot at once. "A great misfortune has struck: Gogol has died in Moscow, died after burning everything, the second volume of *Dead Souls* and a mass of other things both finished and in progress, really everything. It would be hard for you to measure how great is our loss, how cruel and complete. There is no Russian whose heart is not bleeding at this moment. He was more than a simple writer for us: he revealed us to ourselves."[19] And two days later, to the publicist Feoktistov: "I feel that this man's death is hiding something else, I want to penetrate this terrible and sad mystery . . . I feel as though dark, noiseless waves have swept together over my head and I am plummeting, numb and mute, to the depths."[20]

Still stunned by the event, he wrote an obituary: "Gogol is dead! What Russian soul would not be shattered by those three words? He is dead. Our loss is so cruel, so sudden, we are still unable to believe it . . . Yes, he is dead, the man whom we now have the right, the bitter right, to call a great man. The man whose name has defined this period of the history of our literature, the man in whom we take pride as in a national treasure."

There was nothing subversive about this text, but for the police of Nicholas I, any fuss made about any author was suspect. The St. Petersburg censor's office forbade publication of the panegyric. Turgenev then sent it to Moscow. There, a more accommodating censor gave his approval, and on March 13, 1852, the text appeared in the *Moscow Gazette,* under the signature "T . . . v." Soon afterward Turgenev was arrested for "disobedience and violation of the rules of censorship" and interned in the Admiralty Prison. He spent a month there, in very bearable circumstances. He had a cell to himself, good food, champagne, books, and visitors. To divert himself, he studied Polish and wrote a short story, "Mumu," the idea for which was given to him by events that had actually taken place at Spasskoye under the baleful reign of Varvara Petrovna. Pen in hand, he was once again settling his score, this time posthumously, with the woman whose domineering personality had poisoned his youth. His rancor was that of a rebellious weakling; even now when she was in her grave, he could not stop gnawing away at it. In the story, the serf Gerasim is employed as gatekeeper by a power-drunk mistress who bears a striking resemblance to the author's mother. He is a deaf-mute who can express himself only in grunts. The one passion of his life is his bitch Mumu. One day the dog's barking wakes the *barynia* and she orders the animal to be destroyed. Will the gatekeeper resist? No; he obediently goes off to drown Mumu in the river. In Turgenev's mind, this simple little tale was one more protest against serfdom. But the Slavophile Aksakov saw more in it: "It is the personification of the Russian people," he wrote to the author, "its terrifying strength and unimaginable sweetness, its withdrawal into itself and its secrecy, its silence in the face of every exaction, its instinctive uprightness and honesty."[21]

On May 16, 1852, Turgenev was released, but to complete his punishment he was ordered to remove himself to Spasskoye and remain there under surveillance by the local police. "My arrest will probably make it impossible for my book to be published in Moscow,"[22] he wrote to Pauline Viardot. And yet, against all odds, the *Memoirs of a Sportsman* were approved by the censor's office and the book came out early in August 1852. A report by one censor, Volkov, nonetheless drew the attention of the Ministry of Education to the perils of this publication: "I do not think that this can procure any benefit, or even any pleasure, to right-minded readers; on the contrary, such tales leave an unpleasant aftertaste." Nicholas I, feeling that to be warned late was better than never, removed the Moscow censor Lvov from office for permitting the publication of a book in which landowners were seen in so unprepossessing a light; but by that time the *Memoirs of a Sportsman* had already made a name for themselves. They were so successful, in fact, that the first edition sold out in a few months, and all major Russian writers of the day paid homage to the mastery of their author. Enthusiastic letters piled up on his desk. They made him happy but did not turn his head. "I am glad the book has come out," he wrote to Annenkov. "It seems to me that with it, to borrow the textbook phraseology, I shall have *added my mite to the treasure* of Russian literature. I have just reread the *Memoirs* myself; many things are pale and scrappy, many are only hinted at, some are wrong, or overdone or underdone; but others are accurate and right and these are the ones that will save the whole book. It is still a long way from a perfect work of art, and one need only reread one of the masters whose brush flows so swiftly and freely to realize what a little pipsqueak one is oneself. I have been reading Molière these last few days. Take any play, say, *Pourceaugnac.* The force, verve, freshness, the grace of the play literally flung me to the ground with my face in the dirt. After that, the quill drops from one's fingers."[23]

Nevertheless, it did not occur to him to drop his own quill in reality. On the contrary, he wanted to go farther, mount higher in the hierarchy of literary creation. As a genre, the short story seemed worn out and finished. What next? A novel? Why not? "We must take a different road," he wrote, again to Annenkov. "We must find it and quit the old path for good. I have struggled long enough extracting essences, triple distillates, from human personalities and pouring them into vials, and saying, 'Uncork and sniff, honorable reader, doesn't that give you a whiff of the true Russian type?' Enough, enough! But here's the real question: am I capable of anything spacious and serene? Shall I be able to draw lines that are simple and clear? Either you'll hear something new from me or you will not hear from me again at all."[24] Annenkov replied, "I am expecting you to produce a novel in which you will have fully mastered all the characters and events and in which you will not be wallowing voluptuously in your own self or in the sudden apparition of the weird creatures of whom you are all too fond."

In his exile at Spasskoye, Turgenev was thinking that perhaps, by condemning him to rustic solitude far from the bustle of the city, the emperor had actually given him a perfect opportunity to create the major work Russia was waiting for.

5

AN ENDURABLE EXILE

At Spasskoye Turgenev turned the big house over to his friends the Tyuchevs—Nicholas Tyuchev was acting as estate manager—and moved into a pavilion. His exile was quiet and comfortable. He walked for hours, read Leo Tolstoy's *Childhood* with enthusiasm, wrote short stories, played chess with Tyuchev, listened to Mrs. Tyuchev's renditions of his favorite songs on the piano, and, from time to time, received a visit from the country police commissioner who was supposed to be keeping an eye on him. This functionary never presumed to advance beyond the entrance hall, accepted a ten-ruble note with bows and scrapes, and withdrew after wishing his "outlaw" a happy continuation of his sojourn in the provinces. The chief activity of the master of the house was hunting. He beat the region, rifle in hand, keeping an exact record of his hunting prowess. "I have shot three hundred and four pieces this year," he proudly wrote to Aksakov, "to be precise: sixty-nine woodcock, sixty-six great snipe, thirty-nine jack snipe, thirty-three capercaillie, thirty-one partridge, twenty-five quail, sixteen hare, eleven water rail, eight moorhen, four duck and a curlew."[1]

In the course of his rambles he visited many villages, got into conversations with the peasants, learned to understand them better, and, while complaining constantly of his solitude, reveled in the

45

charm of the Russian countryside as season followed season. Coming home, he would find his young mistress, the lively, dark-haired Theoctista, ever smiling and well disposed. In the end, though, her docility began to pall. Pauline Viardot had given him a taste for the tantalizing in love, and the fact was that it rather suited him to be tormented by a strong-willed female—his mother had early accustomed him to this form of misery.

In winter, the thought of his isolation began to weigh upon him. Buried in snow, Spasskoye felt as if it were ten thousand miles from civilization, the well-bred murmur of drawing-room conversation, city lights. "What is there left for me?" he wrote to Pauline Viardot. "I think I've told you more than once: work and memories. But to make the former easier and the latter less bitter, I need your letters, with their sounds of a happy, active life, and that perfume of sun and poetry they bring . . . I feel my life leaking away drop by drop, like the water from a faucet someone has forgotten to turn off. I don't want it back; let it all go . . . What should I do with it? It is not given to anyone to go back over the traces of the past, but I am fond of recalling it—so alluring, so impossible to seize hold of—on an evening like tonight when, listening to the doleful howl of the wind over all these snowdrifts, it seems . . . Fie! I'm not going to depress myself, or you either, with my grievances. Everything that is happening to me is perfectly endurable and one must simply straighten one's back in order to lighten the load."[2]

To distract himself, he wrote more short stories, "The Inn," "The Two Friends," and worked on a novel called *Two Generations,* "the material for which," he told Aksakov, "has been fermenting in me for a long time." In this novel, he again tried to use autobiographical material. The central character was a willful and imposing woman, another reincarnation of Varvara Petrovna. The hero, a fickle, changeable, complex man who becomes infatuated with a young companion of his mother out of sheer idleness, had many features in common with the author. But the chapters wouldn't hang together properly, the story was weighted down with digressions, and Turgenev had to admit that he was less at ease on a long run than in the short hops of *Memoirs of a Sportsman.*

Diversions were few at Spasskoye, so he decided to give a fancy-dress ball to celebrate Christmas and the New Year. The servants outdid one another in creating the most comical disguises and masks, and some workers from a local paper mill acted "a private play" so badly and with such self-assurance that Turgenev almost split his sides laughing. When would he ever be able to see a real play again, on a real stage, performed by real actors? Then, all of a sudden, a stupefying piece of news swept into the desert of Spasskoye: Pauline Viardot was coming to Russia for a series of concert recitals.

Turgenev immediately lost his head. Come what may, he had to be with his idol again. Defying the police, he procured himself a false passport and, on March 20, 1853, reached Moscow quivering with hope. He stayed there ten days, meeting the soprano in secret. Their rare encounters, behind closed doors and drawn curtains, disappointed him. There was no doubt about it: Pauline Viardot's feelings had again cooled. Time and distance had transformed love into a courteous friendship. Back at Spasskoye he received two letters from her, so conventional and unforthcoming that he felt as if he had been tossed into an icy bath. "Especially the second one," he said, every word of which seemed to him to be "the last."[3] Yet, less than a month later, he was writing to her: "Do not give up your idea of another series of concerts in Russia next year . . . There is an avenue of tall birches outside my windows; their leaves are still slightly wrinkled, they still show traces of the sheath, the bud in which they were wrapped only a few days ago; it gives them a party look, as though they had on a brand new frock in which one can still see some wrinkles in the material. My whole garden is filled with nightingales, orioles, thrushes, what a benediction! If I could think that one day you would walk there! It is not impossible . . . but it is also not very likely."[4]

Despite this last affirmation of affection, the correspondence between Turgenev and Pauline Viardot waned in the ensuing months. He no longer felt the need to tell her every detail of his life and cry out his love in the wilderness. Soon after, he also tired of Theoctista Volkov and broke off with her, but not without rewarding her liberally for her good and loyal services.

As the autumn began to fade, the prospect of another winter in the back of beyond at Spasskoye sent him into a panic, and he wrote a plea to General Dubelt for permission to go to St. Petersburg: "Eighteen months ago it was my misfortune to incur the wrath of His Imperial Majesty and, in consequence of a higher decision, I find myself in compulsory residence in the country."[5] As grounds for his application, he gave ill health and the need to consult competent physicians. On November 23 an announcement finally came, from Count Orlov, director of gendarmes and head of the Third Section, that he would thereafter be permitted to reside in the capital. Giddy as a newly released convict, he prepared to quit the endearing haunts of his exile. "I am happy to return to the common rut,"[6] he wrote to Annenkov.

His friends on the staff of the *Contemporary* gave a sumptuous banquet in his honor, and more banquets followed. Restored to city life, Turgenev's figure shone in every drawing room, tall, massive, elegant, graying; he threw his money away in fistfuls. He was now living in a luxurious furnished apartment and had a valet, Zachary, and a noted cook named Stephan, for whom he paid a small fortune. His table was permanently open; every evening he entertained his colleagues on the *Contemporary*—Nekrasov, Panayev, Grigorovich, Annenkov, Druzhnin, Polonsky, Botkin; together they composed impertinent epigrams that made the rounds of the town.

When spring came, his heartstrings began tugging again. He started paying regular visits to the home of one of his cousins, Alexander Turgenev, whose eighteen-year-old daughter Olga was a picture of grace, intelligence, and virginal shyness. Touched by so much freshness, Turgenev could not hide his emotion from her, and she was not indifferent to the attention being lavished upon her by such a mature man, a man with silver temples and a languishing gaze. He saw her often in her parents' villa at Peterhof. Their conversations had a suave and melancholic tone; as visit succeeded visit, he began to think almost seriously of marrying her. But the idea of binding his life to a woman, however pretty and well brought up, intimidated him. He was born to sigh after unattainable heights, not content himself with the meager broth of the happily married couple. He mentioned these contradictory leanings to a few friends. Old Aksakov even read his fortune in the cards for him.

Suddenly he decided to back off. In the letter to Olga that terminated their relationship he accused himself of lacking foresight: "I alone am guilty. I am older than you and my duty was to think for both of us. I did not have the right to let myself be carried away by unconscious feelings . . . before realizing clearly what the nature of those feelings was. I did not have the right to forget that you had much to lose, and I nothing . . . When I was convinced that my feelings were beginning to change and weaken I went on behaving badly in regard to you . . . Despite all that has happened, I consider my relationship with you one of the happiest events of my life. Now, my duty is to avoid seeing you often and having any close relations with you. We must put a stop to the rumors and gossip to which my behavior has given free rein."[7]

The girl was deeply affected by this about-face; as for Turgenev, he thought of her a few years later when he was creating Tatyana, the jilted fiancée of the hero of his novel *Smoke*. But for the present, he was mostly happy to have put an end to an idyll that was poetic enough, no doubt, but that, if it went on any longer, might well end with him standing at the altar.

Soon afterward he became involved with the wife of one of his neighbors in the country, who happened to be none other than Leo Tolstoy's sister Marya.* "She is charming, intelligent and simple, I could not take my eyes off her," he wrote Annenkov. "Despite my advanced years (I was thirty-six four days ago), I almost fell in love . . . I cannot hide from you the fact that I have been fairly smitten. It is a long time since I have met so much grace, so much affecting seductiveness . . . I do beg you will keep this to yourself."[8]

His passion for Marya was also to remain platonic; but, following what had by now become a habit, he used the young woman later in the character of Vera in his story in nine letters, "Faust." In the meantime, he was publishing other stories: "The Region of Dead Calm," "The Nightingales," "A Correspondence," and so on. Then, suddenly emboldened, he launched into a novel. This was not *Two Generations,* which he had abandoned, but a new project, to which he was deeply attached: *Rudin.* The first draft was completed in seven weeks, and the ink was hardly dry on the manuscript before Turgenev began reading it to his regular literary advisers, Botkin, Nekrasov, and Panayev. Their overall response was positive, but they suggested a few improvements that the author hastened to adopt. He was happy to have given birth to a real novel at last, with a complete plot and rounded, subtle characters.

Dmitri Rudin, the hero, is another "superfluous man," eloquent, sparkling, all words and gesticulations, but incapable of sincere emotion. Introduced into a circle of rich landowners, his aura and fluency seduce the women while the men envy and distrust him. Natalya, the daughter of the house, soon falls victim to his allure and is prepared to go to any lengths to marry him. But when Natalya's mother announces that she objects to the marriage, the ostensibly self-confident Rudin collapses like a burst balloon. His love is not strong enough to force a decision. The very thought of making choices turns his blood to ice. Having no will of his own, he drifts as the breeze blows him. He spurns the girl's candid passion and writes her a letter breaking off the relationship that is very like the one the author wrote to Olga

*She married another Tolstoy, Valerian Petrovich.

Turgenev: "Dear Natalya, I have decided to leave. There is no other way out for me." In an epilogue, written a few years later, the reader is informed that Rudin was killed on June 26, 1848, in Paris, on the barricades. "Hey," one of the fleeing rebels says to another, "they've just got the Pole!"

Turgenev's intimates recognized many features of Bakunin in the character of Dmitri Rudin: his build for one, and his mane, his gestures, his habit of sponging off his friends, and the intellectual fire and eloquence that never committed the whole of himself. After some beating about the bush, Turgenev confessed that he had indeed had Bakunin in mind when writing the book. But in reality, he had primarily been thinking of himself. He had observed in his own behavior that same mixture of verbal exaggeration and inner paralysis, the need to be attractive to women and the fear of being entrapped by any one woman, the superficial agitation that went hand in hand with extreme prudence. In portraying Dmitri Rudin he had been denouncing his own weaknesses, indulging in a touch of self-flagellation; and as he was by nature something of a masochist, the punishment did not really make him suffer. Dmitri Rudin, fed on his author's blood, is indisputably believable. The reader, initially attracted to this fine specimen of the Russian intelligentsia, gradually discovers his pettiness and condemns him as contemptible, though he is finally compelled to pity him too. After finishing the book, the reader is left with the enigma of a human soul. Who was Rudin? Turgenev did not judge him. He presented every facet of the character, without comment. This technique was sufficiently new in itself to earn the respect of discriminating readers. They were perfectly aware that with *Rudin* a new, modern breath was blowing into the world of literature.

There was also the style, an infallible elegance and musical sensitivity, a pure language reminiscent of Pushkin's, but more colorful, more sensual—a supple, smooth prose capable of accurately rendering every shade of psychological or physical meaning. A prose that dilated your eyes, nostrils, ears, mouth, and heart, a prose that dropped you into the very midstream of life. Nekrasov, commenting on the behavior of the idealistic visionary Rudin, wrote that Turgenev had presented in his novel "a type of individual who even a short time ago could be found at the forefront of that movement of life and thought whose enthusiasm was captivating an ever wider, ever more important portion of our society." He concluded, "These people had a profound significance and have left deep and fertile traces. Despite their weak and silly sides, we cannot help respecting them."[9]

Naturally, Turgenev read the book to Marya Tolstoy, who praised it lavishly. He was seeing her often, for the pleasure of both looking at and prattling to her. One of their subjects of conversation was her brother Leo, a young author of talent who was then serving as an artillery officer at the front. The Crimean war had broken out in March 1854, but the military operations were so far from the capital that Turgenev could not really take them seriously. He thought it a meaningless conflict, a brainchild of politicians and military chiefs of staff that had no real bearing on the future of the peoples concerned. Of course he deplored the needless deaths and the fact that France and England were opposing Russia, and he longed for the slaughter to end quickly so that he could resume his travels in Europe. But his letters were not laden with patriotic reflections. What annoyed him most about the situation was the publication in Paris of his *Memoirs of a Sportsman* under the title, *Mémoires d'un seigneur russe ou Tableau de la situation actuelle des nobles et des paysans dans les provinces russes* [*Memoirs of a Russian Aristocrat, or, Portrait of the Present Condition of Nobles and Peasants in the Russian Provinces*]. This phrase, he said, made his stories sound as if they were meant to be anti-Russian propaganda. In the St. Petersburg *Gazette,* he protested against the book's misinterpretation by French critics. As a lover of France, he suffered from the wave of anti-Russian feeling that had risen in that country with the beginning of the military campaign.

The death of Nicholas I on February 18, 1855, at the most critical moment of the siege of Sebastopol, and the subsequent accession of Alexander II, gave him hopes that a peace would soon be signed. But the war dragged on, fierce and bloody. National feeling intensified on both sides; Turgenev, the enemy of every form of fanaticism, found himself alone in his neutrality. After the fall of Sebastopol on August 27, 1855, the exhausted Russian army retreated to the north shore of the bay. Leo Tolstoy was in the front line. Turgenev had been much impressed by his articles on the heroic resistance of the besieged, and sent him a letter of encouragement: "Your sister must have written to tell you what a high opinion I have of your talent and what expectations I have of you . . . But I dislike to think of you where you are now. Although in a way I am glad you are having these new impressions and experiences, there is a limit to everything . . . You have shown sufficient proof of your bravery, but the military life is not for you . . . Your weapon is the pen, not the sword."[10] He invited his young colleague to call on him as soon as he had a furlough.

On November 21, 1855, Leo Tolstoy turned up at his door

unannounced. He was just back from the front, in uniform, his face tough and tanned, his gaze proud.[11] An enthralled reader of the *Memoirs of a Sportsman,* he had wanted to meet their author at once. When he first found himself in front of the tall, thick, soft man with the silver hair and carefully groomed side whiskers, large weak hands, and tender woman's eyes, he felt a surge of delight, as if he were looking at a father and friend. Turgenev immediately invited him to be a guest in his apartment, assigned him sleeping quarters, covered him with praise, showed him off to his colleagues on the *Contemporary.* All of them eagerly adopted the bashful, high-headed hero of twenty-seven who had just returned from hell and was majestically ignorant of the literary squabbles of the capital.

Tolstoy's crude manners soon got on Turgenev's nerves, however. The two men had not one thing in common. Turgenev took great pains with his dress, used scent, was fond of fine linen, order, cleanliness, and trifling with the ladies. Tolstoy wore his clothes any which way, smelled of tobacco, never put anything away, sneered at drawing-room conversation, spent his time in gypsy cabarets, and quite liked being taken for a hardened veteran. In discussions with friends Turgenev was always conciliating and attentive to his opponent's arguments; he wanted to see the human condition improved through a peaceful evolution of customs. Tolstoy opposed the majority view with the vehemence of a Roman orator and thought that salvation could come only from an immediate and total upheaval of European civilization. Turgenev was a man of subtleties, hesitations and compromise, Tolstoy a man of primary colors, systematic contradiction, all or nothing. Turgenev considered himself an artist. Tolstoy already saw himself as a project.

Quarrels between the two became frequent. Tolstoy was no longer living with Turgenev, but they often had occasion to meet in the homes of mutual friends. They disputed publicly on any and every issue. To Turgenev, faint with fury, Tolstoy would observe, dryly, "I refuse to believe that your words express real conviction. Here I stand, a dagger or sword in my hand, and I say, 'So long as I live no one shall enter this room!' Now, that is a conviction. But all you do, all of you, is try to hide your real thoughts from each other, and you call that a conviction!" "Then why do you come here among us?" Turgenev cried, his voice shrill with anger. "This is not the place for you." "I don't need you to tell me where to go!" Tolstoy retorted. "And it isn't my presence here or anywhere else that is going to change your empty chatter into real convictions."[12]

One time, after another of these wild and senseless arguments, Nekrasov came over to Tolstoy, who was slouched on a sofa, and said in a placating tone, "Tolstoy, my dear fellow, don't get yourself so worked up. You know how much Turgenev loves and respects you!" Rising up on one elbow, nostrils flaring in rage, Tolstoy retorted, "I shall not permit him to go on eternally doing everything he can to provoke me. Look at him now, pacing up and down, deliberately waggling his democratic thighs in my face."[13] A few days later, at a dinner at Nekrasov's, Tolstoy was teasing Turgenev about his admiration for George Sand. To hear him, the French woman novelist's heroines deserved to be "lashed to the hangman's cart and dragged through the streets of St. Petersburg." When Turgenev tried to protest, Tolstoy battered him down with sarcasm in front of the assembled company. "I nearly quarreled with Tolstoy," Turgenev wrote to Botkin. "Lack of breeding will always out, one way or another. The argument grew very heated. The upshot of it was that he disgusted us all and showed himself in his worst light."[14] Tolstoy was also recording the turbulent installments of this love-hate relationship in his diary: "February 7 1856. Quarreled with Turgenev." "February 13. Dined at Turgenev's. We made it up again." "March 23. Quarreled with Turgenev, this time for good, I think." "April 25. Went to Turgenev's, with pleasure." "May 5. I insulted everyone . . . Turgenev left. I am depressed." Five days later he was writing to his kinswoman Tatyana Ergolskaya, "He [Turgenev] is gone and I feel that I was beginning to care for him a great deal, even though we did nothing but argue. Without him, I am perishing of boredom."[15]

Turgenev, his nerves stretched to breaking point, had fled to Spasskoye to work in the soft loveliness of the Russian spring. By then the war had ended, with the signing of the treaty of Paris. He was going to be able to think about literature again without a bad conscience. He was also going to be able to dream of a trip abroad. For Turgenev, the first consequence of the cessation of hostilities was the right to return to Pauline Viardot. He hadn't seen her for years, they virtually never wrote any more, and yet she was the only person in the world who mattered to him. He wanted to be with her again. Not to conquer her, he had no desire for victory; but to endure her, to serve her, to adore her with the docility of a pet animal. When he applied for his passport to France he knew full well how much he was leaving behind: his house at Spasskoye, the Russian countryside, his friends in St. Petersburg and Moscow, the possibility of marrying and having a family; but he was in the grip of a mirage and it was pulling at him harder every day. He eagerly analyzed his complex feelings in conversation with a new friend, Countess Elisabeth Lambert, a cultivated and pious woman whose husband was one of the emperor's aides de camp. She would receive him alone in a room lined with icons and piled high with books, and she positively hung on his words as he discoursed upon the state of his soul. "Ah, countess!" he wrote to her from Spasskoye, "there is nothing more ridiculous than this craving for happiness, when one has ceased to believe in happiness!"[16] Further on, "At my age, going abroad means resigning myself to a nomad's life for good, sacrificing all plans for a family life. But what can I do about it? Surely, this must be my destiny. As it happens, people who lack strength of character like to pretend they have destinies. It saves them the trouble of making any effort of will and taking responsibility for themselves. In any event, *le vin est tiré, il faut le boire* [the wine is drawn and must be drunk]."* He added, "I personally no longer look forward to happiness for myself . . . When I cast an eye over my life thus far I observe that absolutely all I have done, or so it seems to me, is to carry on a wild goose chase. At least Don Quixote believed in the beauty of his Dulcinea; whereas our modern Quixotes clearly see that their Dulcineas are plain as pikestaffs, and still they chase after them."[17]

An odd confession to make on the eve of his departure for France; implicitly, he was acknowledging that his Dulcinea-Viardot was no beauty—but her flair, her poise, her fire, and her talent made every other mistress he had or might have had in her absence pale into insignificance. Himself an impenitent Don Quixote, he was about to embark upon yet another campaign, although he was virtually certain of defeat before he started. To be miserable by her side seemed a more enviable fate, though, than to be happy with somebody else. Secretly he may even have been hoping for the delectable torture of scorn, rejection, indifference.

Thanks to Count Lambert's influence, he was granted a passport for travel abroad, and set out. After leaving Spasskoye on July 11, 1856, he spent a few days with Nekrasov at Oranienbaum and then, on July 21, in St. Petersburg, boarded a ship bound for Stettin.

*In French in the original.

6

PERCHED ON THE
EDGE OF ANOTHER
BIRD'S NEST

Six years had elapsed since Turgenev's last trip outside Russia. Then he had been a sort of amateur literary hanger-on, idle and impecunious, fleeing the wrath of his mother. Now his mother was dead, he had inherited a substantial fortune, and was recognized in his homeland as an author of the first rank. The *Memoirs of a Sportsman,* other short stories published subsequently, and more recently *Rudin* had ensured him the esteem of a wide readership, and even the most difficult critics were agreed as to the quality of his writing. People said that Tsar Alexander II had actually wept while reading the *Memoirs.* From the outside, then, Turgenev's life looked like a success; but he contemplated his own future glumly and with bitterness.

The ship he sailed on reminded him of his first trip at sea, with the difference that this time there was no fire and he could play lansquenet and whist without the exhortations of Varvara Petrovna prodding at his remorseful mind. The game that really mattered to him, though, was a far different one. He was very much aware that in going abroad he had staked everything he had on the single card that had Pauline Viardot's face on it; and that card was by no means in his hand.

From Stettin he traveled overland to Berlin, from Berlin to Paris, and from Paris to London to meet Herzen, who had been expelled

55

from France for contributing to Proudhon's *La Voix du peuple*. The ebullient revolutionary questioned him eagerly about the trend of people's attitudes in Russia, and Turgenev made an effort to inform him impartially, denouncing the government's faults but stressing the liberal schemes that the new emperor was said to be planning to launch. Then he made his pilgrimage to Courtavenel, where Pauline Viardot and her husband joined him.

The meeting was both affecting and embarrassed. With her broad shoulders, protruding eyes, and wide mouth, the flesh-and-blood Pauline could hardly fail to fall short of the glorified edifice Turgenev's imagination had constructed in her absence. But still, a sort of magic emanated from her that he was quite unable to resist. He quickly fell into her power once again, and for a few weeks he was perfectly happy. He hunted with the husband and probably slept with the wife. To entertain themselves in the evenings, they also played music, read aloud, or acted plays with guests. "How delightfully we spent the time at Courtavenel!" he wrote to Botkin. "Every day seemed like a gift."[1]

But he fretted, as he put it himself, to find himself "perched on the edge of another bird's nest." His friend Fet, the poet, came to visit him in the "nest," and Turgenev described his distress to him: "I am governed by that woman's will. In my eyes she has long since obliterated everything else forever. I deserve what I am getting . . . I am happy only when some woman has her heel on my neck and is grinding my face into the mud." Then, wringing his hands, he moaned, "Good Lord, what a blessing it is for a woman to be ugly!"[2] What he resented most in Pauline Viardot was her impassiveness; he meanwhile shook and shuddered in the storm. She was as motherly to him as she was to her husband; no doubt she played them both false when on tour. The truth was that her art and career mattered so much to her that no man's passage through her life could really disturb its course. In her company, Turgenev sometimes felt as if he were a sort of marshmallow dangling from an iron hook.

Another source of concern for Turgenev was his daughter, Paulinette, now fourteen. She had quite forgotten her mother tongue, could not even say "bread" or "water" in Russian, warbled French like a native of Île-de-France and could rattle off whole passages of Molière and Racine. This delighted Turgenev. "Why should she remember the language of a country to which she will never return?"[3] he wrote to Botkin. But it worried him that the girl got along so badly with her benefactress. The air between Pauline Viardot and his daughter was charged with electricity. Tiffs were frequent. Paulinette had probably sensed the truth of the relationship between her father and Pauline Viardot. And Louise, the eldest daughter, disliked the little intruder and made her feel the full ambiguity of her position in the family.

To prevent the situation from deteriorating further, Turgenev took Paulinette to live in Paris. First they stayed at 206, rue de Rivoli, then at 11, rue de l'Arcade. An English governess was engaged to look after the child's education. Turgenev's feelings for Paulinette were a mixture of affection and compassion, but there was also a constant, nagging sense that his determination to "do right" by her was somehow strained, artificial. The truth is that a man so torn between literature and love could not comfortably play the part of father. Pauline Viardot did not satisfy him, and neither did his work. He complained to his friends that he had lost the desire to write. An eternal malcontent, he longed for Russia at the same time as he was proclaiming himself happier in France. "Whatever else one may say about it," he confided to Botkin, "my Russia is dearer to me than anything else. I feel it most when I am abroad."[4] He was impatient for news of his colleagues in St. Petersburg and Moscow. Tolstoy had written, so he answered, in a letter in which he tried to analyze their stormy relationship: "You are the only man in the world with whom I have had misunderstandings and they arose precisely because, with you, I did not want to remain within the limits of a simple friendship. I wanted to go further and deeper . . . We have little in common. Your whole life is facing forward, mine is built on the past. It is impossible for me to follow you. And nor can you fall in with me. You're too far from me, and you are also too solidly planted on your own feet to become a disciple of anything . . . In a word, we will never be friends in the Russian sense, but we will love each other and rejoice in each other's success."[5]

Turgenev's mood was further darkened by a painful kidney complaint. He consulted numerous physicians, sampled and discarded various medicines, swallowed quantities of quinine. He had begun *A Nest of Gentlefolk* [more recently translated as, among others, *Home of the Gentry*] but let it drop, feeling sick and unsure of his powers. Yet his latest book, *Short Stories and Tales,* had been published with great *éclat* in St. Petersburg, and response to his "Faust" was excellent. But that was the past. And he was wondering whether, with his health so precarious and his energy so low, he would be able to go on at all. He thought of his father, who had died young of a kidney stone. No doubt he was condemned to end the same way. With every sneeze he foresaw the worst. It was very cold in Paris, his heating was inadequate. Seated in front of the only fire in his apartment, he shivered and cursed. Why on earth had he gone there? Even the French writers had become stale. He went to Madame d'Agoult's *salon* and met Victor Hugo, Leconte de Lisle, Lamartine, George Sand herself, but saw them as corks bobbing on the troubled ripples of *la vie parisienne.* "It is all petty, prosaic, empty, and devoid of talent," he wrote to Aksakov. "Lifeless agitation, the tinsel or platitudes of impotence, a complete failure to understand anything that is not French, a total absence of any faith, any conviction, even an artistic conviction—that is what you meet when you look about you . . . Through this noise, this din, can be heard, like the voices of middle-aged singers, the creakings of Hugo, the demented snivelings of Lamartine, the stammers and ramblings of George Sand; Balzac is hailed as an idol and the new school of realists grovels to him on its face in the dust . . . The overall level of morality is falling daily and every person one sees is feverishly grasping for gold; and that is France. If I live here it is not because of France or Paris but because of circumstances that are quite beyond my control."[6]

Those "circumstances quite beyond his control" had a name—Pauline Viardot. She came to see him in his apartment in Paris, but their relations had subsided to the platonic level again. Turgenev's "delicately intimate" ailment no doubt had something to do with this propriety; but beyond that, Pauline had another lover now, the painter Ary Scheffer. All Paris knew about it, and Turgenev endured his disgrace with impotent fury. He cursed his age, his bladder, his physical inadequacy, his solitude: "My bladder is keeping me from writing, disrupting my peace and clarity of mind," he said to Botkin. "I feel unfree. It is as though somebody were holding a candle beneath the sole of my boot, just close enough not to burn the skin."[7] And to the writer Druzhnin, "I am condemned to live as a gypsy and it is plain that I shall never make a nest of my own anywhere."[8] Even Tolstoy was entitled to his despairing confidences: "I am decomposing in this alien air, like a frozen fish in a thaw. I'm too old not to have a nest of my own and stay in it. In the spring I shall come back to Russia without fail, even though in leaving here I must bid farewell to my last dream of what people call happiness, or, to speak more plainly, to the dream of the joy that comes with the sense of satisfaction in a regular life."[9] A few weeks later he confessed to Annenkov,

"She [Pauline Viardot] is the only woman I have ever loved and I shall love her eternally."[10]

She, meanwhile, had a thousand subtle reasons for not wanting to lose Turgenev. He was charming, elegant, and loyal; he was a brilliant conversationalist, had very sound taste in music, and was extremely thoughtful and attentive. She was flattered that a writer of his stature should be so much in her thrall that he could no longer breathe out of her sight. Now that their relationship had been reduced to one of mere affection, she was more conscious than before of the value of his attachment to her.

Turgenev had sunk into such a trough of jealousy and woe that the very idea of a literary career seemed absurd to him. "I shall speak no more of myself," he wrote to Botkin. "I am a man who has gone bankrupt and that's the end of it . . . I am constantly feeling like a bit of rubbish someone has forgotten to sweep up . . . Not one more line of mine will be printed (or written) before the end of this century. Three days ago I didn't burn (not wanting to be accused of copying Gogol) but rather tore up and threw into the toilet everything I had started, outlines etc. Trifles, all of it. I do not have any special form of talent. I did have a poetic string or two but they have already been wrung and fallen silent, and I have no desire to repeat myself. On the shelf! This is no passing fit of pique, believe me, it's the expression or fruit of slowly ripened conviction."[11] In the same letter he told Botkin that Tolstoy had briefly been in Paris: "He looks at everything, stares, doesn't open his mouth. He has become more intelligent but still seems not to know what to do with himself, which means that other people can't be comfortable around him. I contemplate him with delight. Frankly, he is the one bright hope of our literature."[12]

This mixture of admiration and irritation became more intense with every letter to his Russian friends: "Tolstoy has changed considerably for the better, but the creakings and groanings of his internal upheavals have a very bad effect on a man like me, whose nerves are already overstrained," he wrote to Annenkov on February 16/28, 1857. "I cannot establish any lasting friendship with Tolstoy, our views differ too widely," he wrote to Kolbasin on March 8/20 1857. And to Annenkov again, on March 9/21, 1857, he wrote: "No; after all my attempts to get along with Tolstoy, I have had to give it up. We are put together too differently. Whatever I like, he doesn't, and vice versa . . . I don't know how to take him. But he will turn into an outstanding man and I shall be the first to applaud and admire him, from afar." "Tolstoy is showing signs of tolerance and calm. When this new wine has done fermenting, it will be a beverage fit for the gods!" he wrote to Botkin on March 23/April 4, 1857. Tolstoy, meanwhile, was writing to Botkin about Turgenev: "His mental agonies are such as can be felt only by a man endowed with an imagination like his." And to his kinswoman Tatyana Ergolskaya, "His unhappy love affair with Pauline Viardot and his daughter keep him here, in an atmosphere that is very bad for him, and he is pitiful to behold. I should never have thought it possible to love like that."[13]

Tolstoy might feel sorry for Turgenev on Monday, but on Tuesday he would be making mincemeat of him.[14] As in the past in St. Petersburg, he scrupulously recorded every twist and turn in his diary: "Dinner with Turgenev. He is quite simply vain and petty" (February 17/March 1, 1857). "Spent three pleasant hours at Turgenev's" (February 20/March 4). "Spent another pleasant evening with Turgenev and a bottle of wine by the fireside" (February 21/March 5). "Turgenev doesn't believe in anything, that's what's the matter with him. He does not love, he is in love with love" (February 25/March 9). "At dinner I told him something he had never suspected, namely, that I consider him superior to me" (February 26/March 10). "Turgenev is really tiresome. Alas, he has never loved anyone" (March 1/13). "Dropped in on Turgenev. He is a cold, futile person, but clever, and his work is inoffensive" (March 4/16). "Stopped by at Turgenev's. No, I really must keep away from him. I have paid tribute enough to his merits, tried every possible way of making friends with him, but it's no use" (March 5/17). "Turgenev came to see me around five. He looked guilty. What to do? I respect him, I value him, I can even say I love him, but I feel absolutely no warmth for him, and the same is true of him" (March 7/19). To sum it up, "Turgenev is treading water, wallowing about in his woes" (February 18/March 2).

At last, Turgenev steeled himself to flee this sentimental miasma and in May 1857 went to see Herzen in London. He stayed long enough to exchange a few lofty ideas with his host and be introduced to Carlyle, Thackeray, Disraeli, and Macaulay, before hurrying away to Berlin and then to Sinzig near Koblenz, where he went to the hot springs for treatment and, miraculously, began to feel like working again. A little German town, ancient lime trees, neat vineyards, a moon, a Gothic steeple, fair-haired girls strolling in the twilight, the broad waters of the Rhine: This was the tranquil setting Turgenev chose for his short story "Asya." Its heroine was, like Paulinette, the illegitimate daughter of a gentleman and a servant girl. Her upbringing had made her, like Paulinette, into a "young lady." But this one was dreamy and mischievous by turns, a twin of Tatyana in *Eugene Onegin*. She was staying at the spa with her brother Gagin, while the narrator, like the author himself, had taken shelter in this backwater to escape from a heartless and fickle woman. "I was seeking solitude," he said. "My heart had just been broken by a young widow . . . At first she lured me on, then hurt me cruelly by dropping me for a red-cheeked Bavarian lieutenant." Pauline Viardot was ever-present, even between the lines of his story. An idyll quickly sprang up between the narrator and Asya, with all the ingredients of German romantic poetry (ruins, sunsets, moonlight, and murmuring streams). At the end, the hero tries, but fails, to make up his mind to ask the young woman to marry him. Her pride hurt, she and her brother depart without warning, leaving a note for her vacillating suitor: "Farewell, we shall not meet again. It is not vanity that makes me go, no, but I cannot do otherwise. If you had said one word to me yesterday when I was weeping in front of you, I should have stayed." And the despairing narrator concludes, "I have known other women since, but the emotion aroused in me by Asya, that burning, tender, profound emotion, never came again . . . Condemned to the loneliness of a bachelor with no family, I drag out the last of my dull years . . ." The freshness of the story, its smooth, uncluttered style, so measured and harmonious, delighted most of Turgenev's friends. Many readers praised the author's psychological acumen and the sense of poetry that shone in his descriptions of landscapes. Some, however, such as the Tyuchevs, found the character of Asya artificial. And Tolstoy said, in a letter to Nekrasov, "In my opinion, it's the weakest thing he has written yet."[15] Turgenev himself was not satisfied with it. "And yet," he told Tolstoy, "I wrote it with much feeling, I almost had tears in my eyes."[16]

He was still at Sinzig when he heard on July 24, 1857, that Pauline Viardot had had a son, Paul.* This was her fourth child, preceded by three girls, Louise (1841), Claudie (1852), and Marianne (1854). But who was its father? In view of his relations with its mother nine months before, Turgenev might feel himself triumphantly responsible for this miracle, and many people were convinced that he was.† He gave free rein to his elation in a letter to the happy

*Paul Viardot was born on July 20, 1857.
†Turgenev specialists have not been able to reach a firm decision; but most believe he was the boy's father, and the descendants of the Viardot family are inclined to think so too.

mother: "Hurrah! Hurrah! *Lebe hoch! Vivat! Evviva Zito!* Long live little Paul! Three cheers for his mother!"[17] And he begged her to tell him, as soon as she could, every circumstance and detail of this event that had made him quite giddy with joy—forgivable, he said, in a man of his age and situation. He must have hoped that this birth would bring him closer to Pauline Viardot. She, however, showed no signs of a sentimental revival where he was concerned. A fulfilled mother and adulated artist, she turned a regal cold shoulder on her valetudinatian suitor.

It suddenly seemed to him that the treatment he was undergoing at Sinzig was doing him no good after all. "The waters here are bad for me," he wrote to Countess Elisabeth Lambert. "I feel unwell. I must leave. But to go where? I have not the least idea myself."[18] Hoping to improve his health, he went to Boulogne and bathed in the sea. He felt no better. He then decided that the only thing that could cure him, physically and emotionally, was a stay at Courtavenel. His reception there was chilly. After raving over the infant who may or may not have been the fruit of his affair with its mother, he began to have the disagreeable sensation that he was one too many in the household. Perhaps it had been a mistake to intrude upon his friends in the midst of their connubial bliss. Pauline was often away. To console himself, he went hunting with her husband. "As you see, I am here," he wrote to Nekrasòv. "That is, I have done the very foolish thing you warned me against. But it was impossible for me to do otherwise. Besides, the result of this foolish thing will be that I shall probably return to Petersburg sooner than planned. No, it's not possible to live like this! I've had enough of perching on the edge of another bird's nest! If one doesn't have a nest of one's own, then one should do without."[19]

He did eventually hop off "another bird's nest" but not, as he had originally thought, to fly to Russia; instead, he went to Italy with Botkin, who had joined him a short time before. They started in Rome. Finding himself again in the city he had first seen seventeen years before, in his student days, Turgenev gloomily compared his youthful zestfulness with the weariness, anxiety, and hopelessness he felt today. His life was that of a wealthy, graying, forty-year-old vagabond with no home port, no roots, no family, and, spurned by the only woman whose days and nights he would have cared to share, his thoughts were turning increasingly to the grave. Nevertheless, he toured the museums and ruins, roamed the countryside, tunneled about in the catacombs, raved over the great paintings, and discussed art with a new friend, the painter Ivanov. Pauline Viardot was not answering his letters. He complained to his daughter, Paulinette: "I conjure you to write the moment you get my letter and tell me about Mme Viardot. I was hoping to find a letter from her on my arrival here [in Rome] but it would seem that the absent are always wrong!"[20]

Since Pauline Viardot seemed to want to persist in her stony silence, he fell back on friends in Russia, relating his torments to them. "My soul is so weighted down and bitter that it is impossible for me to describe my state to you," he wrote Annenkov. "Work alone could save me, but if that does not go well, all is lost. I have wasted my life on trivia."[21] To Countess Lambert, "There are moments of sudden change in our lives, when the past dies and something new begins . . . Soon I shall be forty. My first, second and even third youths have flown. It is time I became, if not a practical man, at least a man who knows where he is going and what goal he hopes to achieve. I cannot be anything but a man of letters; although thus far I have been primarily a dilettante. But things will be very different hereafter."[22]

He was inspired by the Eternal City to live up to his word. On December 22, 1857, he told Countess Lambert that he had started to write "a long short story in which the chief character is a profoundly pious young woman." The long short story turned into the novel started in Paris, *A Nest of Gentlefolk* [or *Home of the Gentry,* etc.]. The work went well and happily—an invocation of Russian landscapes, Russian faces, and Russian life amid the noble Roman stones. Perhaps this new work would repay all the emotional agonies he had endured during his latest travels? "I knew before setting out on this trip abroad that it would be very bad for me," he wrote in the same letter. "I knew I should do better to stay home. I knew and yet I went."[23] In the spring of 1858 he left Rome with his novel unfinished and moved on to Florence, Vienna, Dresden, Leipzig, and London, where he saw Herzen again. The revolutionary was now editing a review, *The Bell,* in which the imperial government was fiercely criticized. Copies were being smuggled into Russia. The two men held impassioned discussions about the schemes for the reform of the status of serf peasants that Alexander II was hoping to introduce. Turgenev, an enthusiastic supporter, trusted to the Tsar's wisdom and generosity, while Herzen was suspicious of the entire Russian nobility. The whole of Russia was buzzing: all the more reason to hurry home.

Around mid-June Turgenev was at Spasskoye again. His friend Fet came to join him. They went hunting together, tramping joyously for days on end in every wind and weather. Sunbaked and rain-soaked, the marksmen carried on their rivalry in slaughter, and when their knees buckled with fatigue they collapsed into a haystack to rest for a few hours. Afterward they would heave themselves upright, unfettered and merry in the middle of some field, and gnaw on a chicken wing. Russia blew into their faces the breath of her fields and forests. Back in the house they would work, each in his room. Hunting, long evenings in front of a book, literary discussions with wineglass in hand—it was an ideal atmosphere in which to finish the first draft of his *Nest of Gentlefolk*. Sometimes Turgenev would flee Spasskoye and call on Tolstoy at Yasnaya Polyana. For a little distraction, he would pay court to Tolstoy's sister Marya, who took his sighs and rolling eyes for the real thing. Tolstoy angrily noted in his diary, "Ivan Turgenev is too much to put up with . . . He is behaving badly to Marya. Swine!"[24] Turgenev, meanwhile, was writing to Botkin, "I'm through with Tolstoy. He has ceased to exist for me . . . If I eat a bowl of soup and like it, I know by that fact alone and with absolute certainty that Tolstoy will find it bad, and vice versa."[25]

He also saw Tolstoy at meetings of the Assembly of Nobility. The imminent emancipation of the serfs, now proclaimed by the tsar, was causing a great ferment in the minds of the landowners. They were afraid that part of their land would be taken away and given to the peasants for some token compensation. As a committed opponent to serfdom since early youth, Turgenev was impatient to see the agrarian reform come into effect at last, while Tolstoy seemed in less of a hurry to liberate his serfs. He was liberal-minded, all right, but his loyalties were still on the side of the owners.

In midsummer, while at Spasskoye, Turgenev learned of the death of the painter Ary Scheffer, his more fortunate rival for the affections of Pauline Viardot. He wrote a dignified letter of condolence: "I did not dare tell you my presentiments, and tried to persuade myself that everything might turn out for the best—and now he is no more. I miss him for his own sake, I miss everything that disappeared with him, and I am deeply conscious of the cruel pain this loss must be to you and of the void which it will be very hard for you to fill . . . I do not pretend to offer any consolation, only a friendly hand outstretched, and a truly devoted heart which says that you may rely upon it as upon the one that has just ceased to beat."[26]

On October 27, 1858, he wrote the last words of his novel *A Nest of Gentlefolk*. Two months later he presented it to a group of friends, including Nekrasov, Annenkov, Pisemsky, and Goncharov. He was recovering from a bad case of bronchitis and couldn't read himself so Annenkov read it for him. It took two evenings. On the whole, his friends' reactions were favorable, although Annenkov criticized a few things and Goncharov drew attention to some suspicious similarities between the manuscript and his own novel *The Precipice,* the outline of which he had once shown to Turgenev. Turgenev gave no explanations but made all the changes needed to pacify his hairsplitting colleague. In response to the charge of plagiarism he later wrote a letter justifying himself to Goncharov. "What would you have me do? I can't go on rewriting the *Memoirs of a Sportsman* forever! And I don't want to stop writing altogether . . . Take me as I am or don't take me at all; but don't demand that I change, and above all don't take me for some sort of Talleyrand. Anyway, that's enough of that! All this fuss gets nobody anywhere. We'll all die and we'll all stink when we're dead!"27

The plot of *A Nest of Gentlefolk* is slight. Lavretsky, the hero, aging and blasé—an almost photographic portrait of the author—takes his wife to Paris, where she becomes the mistress of a twenty-three-year-old French lady-killer. Having learned of her betrayal, the disenchanted and disgusted Lavretsky abandons his faithless spouse and quickly forgets that she ever existed: "Lavretsky was not born to be a martyr; his healthy nature soon reclaimed its rights." Returning to Russia, he meets a girl, Liza, in the home of some friends, and is instantly subjugated by the pure, pious, spontaneous young woman. It seems to him that his life is accelerating, taking a new turn. At the height of his infatuation he learns from an item in a Paris review that his wife has died. Freed, he declares his love to the girl, and she reciprocates. They decide to get engaged. But the death notice was a mistake. The repudiated wife suddenly turns up and presents Lavretsky with a little girl whose father, she says, is Lavretsky himself. With abject cunning she implores his forgiveness and begs for a place in the household. Lavretsky refuses to live with her again; but Liza, heartbroken, retires to a convent.

On the basis of this trite and melodramatic plot Turgenev built a delicate, human, profound novel. The narration of a joy that is destroyed almost as soon as it is born is enveloped in poetic charm. Further, the whole book is steeped in the calm radiance of the Russian countryside. We see it by night and by day, shimmering, scented, mingling with the characters' moods. *A Nest of Gentlefolk* was an instant hit with readers and critics alike. It was universally agreed that Turgenev had no equal among contemporary Russian writers. At that point, Tolstoy had published nothing but his trilogy *Childhood, Boyhood,* and *Youth,* and a few stories, while Dostoyevsky, after a promising start, was silent, having been exiled to Siberia by order of the late Nicholas I. The way was free. For the first time in years Turgenev could tell himself that literary renown afforded at least some compensation for his heavy heart.

7

LIBERAL
AND NIHILIST

As he drifted in the eddies of Russian intellectual circles, Turgenev was becoming increasingly convinced that his country's salvation lay in prompt reform at home and a comprehensive mixing and merging with Europe. Already, thanks to the courageous initiative of Alexander II, a commission was drafting a plan to abolish serfdom. Censorship was less stringent. The students were agitating, eager to play a part in the overturn of the old régime. The author was wondering how he could embody this modernizing drive in a work of fiction. He too wanted to bear witness to his time. His idea was to show an idealistic young woman breaking with her bourgeois background to follow the career of a strong and resolute man of action. A few years earlier a neighbor of his in the country named Karatayev had left for the front at the start of the Crimean war and gave him, just before his departure, a notebook in which he haltingly recounted his love for a girl who had rejected him. Later, the girl met a Bulgarian patriot, fell in love with him, and followed him to Bulgaria, where he died of tuberculosis.

After years of maturing in his mind, this tale, to which Turgenev had initially attached no importance, now suddenly demanded to be told. At last he had his stalwart hero, the man who could subjugate a free-minded virgin! Rudin had been a "superfluous man," a man of the past; this would be a man of heart, devoted body and soul to a new cause; a man of the present, maybe even the future. Excited by the idea, Turgenev set to work in March 1859, at Spasskoye, on a novel to be called *On the Eve.* He continued it in St. Petersburg, Paris, Vichy, and finally Courtavenel, where he realized, to his pain, that to Pauline Viardot he was no longer anything but an innocuous old friend. "My health is good," he wrote Countess Lambert, "but my soul is sad. I live in the midst of a quiet, orderly family. Why am I here? Why, having broken away from all that was dear to me, am I here looking into the past? You will easily understand what I mean and what my position is. But having said that, I do not suffer overmuch. It is said that a man dies several times before his death. I know what is dead in me. So what is the use of staring at a closed tomb?"[1]

After returning to Russia early in the autumn of 1859, he set about dividing his land into plots for the peasants and deciding on the pittance they were to pay him, without waiting for the land reform to be enacted officially. He polished his manuscript and reread it with mingled satisfaction and apprehension. It was his first "social" novel. At last the Russian maid was escaping from her "nest" and following the iron man who fought for his country's freedom from oppression by the Turks. But where Elena, the Russian girl, could stir the reader with her emotional intensity, Insarov, the iron man, was all speech, hopelessly conventional. At no point in the book does he become anything more than an abstract notion that the author has been unable to bring to life. All one can conclude about the patriot is that he was a hotheaded, obstinate Bulgarian—not enough to give him a semblance of vitality.

When Countess Lambert read the manuscript, she was appalled. Everything in it offended her—and most of all the behavior of Elena, who abandons her family out of love for a political adventurer. Dismayed by the reaction of his best friend, Turgenev's first impulse was to destroy the book. Annenkov dissuaded him. But when *On the Eve* came out in the *Russian Messenger,* criticism poured in from all sides. Conservative newspapers condemned the heroine as amoral and contrasted her with the true Russian woman—pious, discreet, worthy, and respectful of family values. Liberal papers found the hero's actions unconvincing and the Slavophile slant of the whole book entirely too pronounced. The fiercest objections came from the very periodical to which Turgenev was a regular contributor, the *Contemporary.* Still under Nekrasov's leadership, the review had recently taken a sharp turn to the left, following the addition to its staff of a couple of intransigent, insolent youngsters. Modest as always, Turgenev sought to placate them with friendship and advice; but they did not appreciate either the courtesy or the feminine sensitivity of their elder. They thought him obsolete, with his aristocratic airs, his refined elegance, his fluency, connoisseurship, sighs, and ineffectual impulses. He, on the other hand, was pained by their lack of breeding, arrogance, dirty fingernails, and disheveled manes, as well as the subversive theories they were broadcasting in every direction. He was an old-school liberal in collision with the new generation of revolutionary democrats.

The leader of the *Contemporary*'s demolition squad was an ex-admirer of Turgenev, a publicist named Chernyshevsky, who had become so "radicalized" that he could no longer tolerate the "old master's" graceful, measured prose. Also among the iconoclasts was a tubercular young critic of great talent named Dobrolyubov. When Turgenev tried to draw him into friendly conversation, the younger man cut him off with "Ivan Sergeyevich, it bores me to talk to you; so let us stop." When *On the Eve* came out, Dobrolyubov immediately wrote a vindictive article in which he said that Turgenev had been cowardly in his portrayal of the hero, who ought to have been Russian and not Bulgarian, and that in any event a real patriot ought to have been more effective in his fight against "the alien government." Dobrolyubov was obviously criticizing the book not as a novel but from an ideological viewpoint, reproaching its author for having failed to make his character into a full-fledged revolutionary. The manuscript of his article was submitted to Turgenev before publication; he felt badly let down by it and immediately wrote to Nekrasov, "I do entreat you not to print this article; it can bring me nothing but a host of miseries; it is unfair and brutal; I shall not know where to hide if it comes out."[2] What added to Turgenev's indignation was his sense that he had written into *On the Eve* all his faith in that very "new man" who was to regenerate the world. He hated serfdom no less than they; he longed as much as they for a future of equality and justice; he was Herzen's friend as much as they were. But they scornfully rejected him. When would they understand that, in politics at least, his position was absolutely clear-cut, that for all his conciliatory manners, he would never depart from it? He was opposed to solutions that meant bloodshed, yet he could not accept the status quo. He too was looking to the future, perhaps even more than they, however much they called themselves "progressives." At times he wondered whether the only thing they really held against him, unconsciously, was his age.

Dobrolyubov's article came out in the March issue of the *Contemporary*. Others followed in the same vein. A satirical magazine, the *Whistle*, wrote that Turgenev "was tied to the petticoats of a tramp singer"; this stung sharply enough, but a deeper wound was inflicted by a colleague who was then enjoying some renown: Goncharov, repeating the suspicions he had voiced in connection with *A Nest of Gentlefolk*, was now accusing Turgenev of having stolen *On the Eve* from him as well. This time, exasperated by Goncharov's neurotic hypersensitivity, Turgenev demanded an arbitration. The arbitrators, Annenkov, Druzhnin, and Dudyshkin, were deeply embarrassed by the whole affair and left the adversaries to decide for themselves, explaining that the coincidences in the two novels were the product of a "fundamentally Russian" inspiration common to both authors. After this dispute, Turgenev broke off relations with Goncharov.

Meanwhile, he had written a long short story, "First Love," which was published in March 1860 in the *Reading Library*. Its subject is closely autobiographical. Here Turgenev tells the tale of his adolescent infatuation with a young neighbor in the country, Catherine Shakovskoy (Zinaida in the story), which lasts until his discovery that she is his own father's mistress. Everything in the story—situation, characters, setting—follows the historical truth. With its elegant, light style, accurate eye, and choice of revealing detail, the work is a small masterpiece of psychology and poetry. Once again, however, the critics were divided. Some of the more liberal were offended because the story did not treat any of the great political and social issues then beleaguering Russia. Others among the conservatives were outraged by the impropriety of writing about a father and son who were both in love with the same woman, and a young woman who was the mistress of a married man. Countess Lambert told Turgenev that the emperor had read "First Love" to the empress and been delighted by it, then added, "It seems to me that this work is one of your wickednesses; but your manner of doing evil is so irresistible."[3] To which he replied, "I was absolutely not trying to create any effect in writing the story. It was given to me all of a piece by life . . . If anyone were to ask me whether I could consent to have the story destroyed and leave not a trace behind, I should shake my head."[4] Even Louis Viardot, easygoing as he was where his wife's infidelities were concerned, found it offensive to think that an author of Turgenev's quality should indulge himself in so "unhealthy" a piece of writing. "Adultery and yet more adultery, unbridled, glorified!" he wrote. "And who is telling this scandalous tale? His son, worse shame! His own son, who, unlike Noah's children, does not cover his father's drunkenness and nakedness but holds them up for all to see in broad daylight . . . What is the point of expending talent on such a subject?"[5] Most readers, however, were delighted by the blend of innocence and audacity, vice and purity, tenderness and brutality in "First Love."

Turgenev might have continued to exploit the sentimental vein in another novel, but once again he decided that he ought to do something different. Hurt by the jabs of one group of the young intellectuals, he determined that his next book would portray one of those "heroes of our time" who, unlike their elders, were bent on destruction, not building. The title of the new novel was to be *Fathers and Sons*. As usual, he carted the manuscript all over Europe with him, from Spasskoye to London, Courtavenel to Paris.

He was in Paris when he learned of the publication of the imperial manifesto of February 19, 1861, emancipating the serfs. It caused him such joy that although he claimed to have no sense of religion, he attended a thanksgiving service at the Orthodox church. He was eager to get back to Russia and see the thrilling effects of the emancipation with his own eyes, yet he kept hanging about in France on one pretext or another. To Herzen, who took him to task for shillyshallying, he wrote a faintly uneasy letter. "Why rub salt in the wound? What can I do, with a daughter who has to be married? That is why I am still in Paris. But with every thought and all my being, I am in Russia."[6] He begged Annenkov to tell him how people in the Russian countryside were reacting to the shock of emancipation. "Here," he wrote, "the Russian traveling gentlemen are quite beside themselves, all telling each other that they have been robbed."[7]

Finally, on April 21/May 3, 1861, he set out. As soon as he got to Spasskoye he tackled the business of organizing his peasants' lives. Under the new statute every *muzhik* was to own outright his house, the enclosed yard adjoining it, and a piece of land equal to the area he had previously been farming. The state gave the former owner of the land a sum of cash corresponding to the value of that area, to be repaid by the farmers over a period of forty-nine years at a rate of six kopeks for every ruble borrowed, interest and amortization included. Unpaid arbiters of the peace, chosen among the local dignitaries, were to supervise the negotiations. In deciding the size of the holdings to be ceded to the erstwhile serfs, account was to be taken of the nature of the soil, climate, and local custom. For this purpose, Russia was divided into three zones: black or fertile land, infertile land, and steppeland. The system was complicated and unpopular with both the landowners, who thought they were being despoiled of a possession that had been justly handed down to them by their forebears, and the *muzhiks,* who could not see why their masters' lands should not be made over to them *in toto* and without payment of any kind. Turgenev, who had been anticipating an explosion of joy among the latter, was disappointed. Instead of a brotherly drawing-together of liberated serfs and their former masters, he observed a rising tide of mistrust, trickery, and hostility on both sides. Each was trying to get the better of the other. There were bitter disputes over the boundary lines of every clod and hummock of earth. "With my own peasants," Turgenev wrote to his friend Polonsky, "things are not going too badly for the moment, because I give way to them wherever possible. But I already foresee trouble ahead."[8] Smiling sadly, he also said, in a conversation with Polonsky, "One day we shall be sitting behind the house drinking tea. And there, through the garden, will come a mob of peasants. They will take their hats off and bow to the ground. 'Well, brothers,' I shall ask, 'what must it be today?' 'Please forgive us, master,' they will say, 'don't be cross with us. You're a good master and we're very fond of you, the only thing is, you've got to be hanged!' " A little later Annenkov received the following confession from Turgenev: "My concessions to the peasants verge upon the cowardly. But you know yourself what a weird bird is our muzhik. It is sheer madness to put any hope in him, as far as repayment is concerned. Henceforth, all explanations are futile."[9]

Tolstoy had agreed to act as arbiter in negotiating friendly settlements of disputes between masters and peasants.[10] Turgenev asked him over to Spasskoye, and after dinner, as a mark of his trust, showed him the manuscript of *Fathers and Sons,* which he had just finished. After a few pages, travel-weary and weighted down by his meal, Tolstoy nodded off. Turgenev was cut to the quick but kept his hurt feelings to himself. The next day the two men set out for Fet's estate at Stepanovka, seventy versts away. A quarrel broke out at their very first gathering around the samovar. They had been talking about charity. Turgenev rather proudly told them that his daughter, Paulinette, who was being brought up abroad by an English governess named Mrs. Innis, had a fixed sum every month to distribute to "her poor." "Now," he added, "the Englishwoman is insisting that my daughter go in person to fetch any of their clothes that need mending, and then she must mend them herself and take them back to their homes." "And you think that is a good thing?" sneered Tolstoy. "Why, of course! That way, charity comes into direct contact with real poverty!'' ''Well, what I think,'' grumbled Tolstoy, ''is that a little girl got up in a fancy dress with dirty, smelly rags on her knees is putting on a hypocritical farce.'' White with anger, Turgenev stuttered, ''So you think I am not bringing up my daughter properly?'' ''I'm just saying what I think, I make no personal allusions,'' Tolstoy retorted. Fet tried to change the subject, but Turgenev was already standing in front of Tolstoy, wild-eyed and staring. ''One more word and I'll smash your face!'' he yelled. Then, clutching his head in both hands, he rushed into the next room. After a moment, having recovered his self-control, he returned to the dining room and said to Fet and his wife, ''I beg you to forgive my unspeakable behavior, which I most deeply deplore!''[11] After stammering a few words of regret to Tolstoy he left, shamefaced and dismayed, and headed back to Spasskoye.

Tolstoy also took leave of his hosts. But on the road his wrath, which had momentarily abated, got the better of him again. He stopped at Novosyelky, an estate belonging to his friend Borisov, and from there dispatched a servant with orders to ride as fast as his horse would go, carrying an ultimatum to Turgenev: he must either send a written apology that he could ''show to Fet and his wife,'' or come to the stagecoach inn at Bogoslovo, where he, Tolstoy, would be waiting for armed satisfaction. Hurt and humiliated, but also conscious of the absurdity of the situation, Turgenev answered: ''I can but repeat what I considered it my duty to tell you at Fet's: carried away by a surge of involuntary animosity which this is not the place to explain, I offended you, without any provocation on your part, and I apologize. I am ready to repeat my apology in writing and ask your forgiveness once again. What took place this morning is a clear indication that any attempt to bring together two such conflicting personalities as yours and mine is doomed to fail. I perform this duty all the more willingly as this letter will probably mark the conclusion of our relationship.''[12] The conciliatory tone of this missive might have appeased the wrath of the man to whom it was addressed, but by mischance Turgenev sent it to Borisov at Novosyelky, thinking Tolstoy was still there, whereas in fact he had already gone to Bogoslovo and was awaiting the reply to his challenge there. As time passed and no messenger appeared, Tolstoy's rage flared into madness and he wrote a second letter demanding a duel at once—and not merely some parody of a duel where two authors fire a few potshots at each other, taking great care to miss, before ending the evening together over a bottle of champagne. He chose the piace for settling their score (on the edge of the forest of Bogoslovo) and asked Turgenev to be there the next morning, with pistols. At dawn a servant from Novosyelky brought him Turgenev's reply to his first letter; then another man came from Spasskoye with the answer to the second. "I will tell you in all sincerity," Turgenev wrote, "that I should gladly stand up to your pistol-fire if that could unsay my ludicrous words. It is so contrary to the habits of a lifetime for me to have spoken as I did that I can only attribute the incident to the irritation caused by the excessive and unending clash of our opinions on every subject. That is why, in parting from you forever— for events like this cannot be forgotten—I believe it my duty to say once again that you are in the right in this matter, and I in the wrong. I would add that for me the point is not to display courage or a lack of it but to acknowledge your right to call me onto the field, presumably in accordance with the generally accepted rules of duelling (that is, with seconds) and also your right to pardon me. You have made the choice that suited you, I submit to your decision."[13]

With angry jubilation, Tolstoy wrote back, "You are afraid of me, I despise you and want no more to do with you."[14] He then sent both letters to Fet, with a caustic commentary. Turgenev, imagining the quarrel at an end, had already left for Paris when he heard from his friend Kolbasin, a great lover of gossip, that Tolstoy was spreading calumnies about him. Would he never hear the end of this sordid piece of trivia? He felt as if he had a pack of wild dogs yapping at his heels. His initial anger returned. He wrote to Tolstoy, "I hear that you are showing a copy of your last letter around Moscow, and have been calling me a coward because I supposedly refused to fight you, etc. After all I have done to take back the words that escaped me, I regard your conduct as offensive and disloyal and I warn you that I shall not let it pass. When I return to Russia next spring I shall demand satisfaction."[15]

This time Tolstoy felt that the lesson must have been learned. Besides, he was being inclined to Christian charity of late. Switching smoothly from savagery to saintliness, he answered his foe: "Sir, you have termed my letter and conduct disloyal; you have also said that you would punch me in the nose. And I offer you an apology, admit my guilt and refuse your challenge to a duel." Turgenev, having had the last word, wrote Fet asking him to tell Tolstoy that he too was giving up any thought of a duel. "From this day forward, *de profundis* on the whole business!" he concluded. Fet felt that Tolstoy ought to be informed of the terms of this letter; but in the interval Tolstoy's angelic mood had left him. This time the high-caste fop with the graying temples and overwrought nerves who had dared to measure grandeurs with him, and the friends who were trying to make peace between the two of them, were tarred with the same brush. In a frenzy of exasperation he wrote to Fet: "Turgenev is a scoundrel who ought to be thrashed. I beg you to transmit that to him as faithfully as you transmit his charming remarks to me, despite the fact that I have asked you never to speak to me of him again . . . I also beg you not to write to me any more, for I shall not open your letters any more than Turgenev's." For seventeen years Turgenev and Tolstoy were to neither meet nor correspond.

Meanwhile, there was another name on every Russian's lips. Dostoyevsky, back from exile, had already brought out one novel with a splash—*The Insulted and Injured*—and followed it with the tale of his harrowing experiences as a convict in a Siberian prison camp, *The House of the Dead.* He was also editing a review, *Time.* Turgenev had promised to send him a short fantasy, "Phantoms," in the near future. But he worked on it halfheartedly, being almost totally absorbed in finishing his big novel, *Fathers and Sons.* He had invested a great deal in this book, which he thought of as a faithful portrayal of the torments of his conscience in regard to the new direction being taken by the younger generation. Systematically assailed by the more progressive contributors to the *Contemporary,* he had recently broken off relations with the periodical and offered *Fathers and Sons* to Katkov's *Russian Messenger* instead. The manuscript was dispatched on January 24/February 5, 1862. "My novel has been sent to the *Russian Messenger,*" he wrote to Polonsky. "It will presumably come out in the February issue. I am anticipating a dreadful beating but I don't really care about that one way or the other."[16]

Throughout *Fathers and Sons,* he had tried to be impartial. His main idea was that an artist should not set out to prove anything—he could show, suggest, light the way, but not pass judgment upon his characters' personalities or acts. This time the subject of his book was dramatically timely. It set out to present the inflexible attitudes of two generations separated by a sea of misunderstanding. On one side are the sons: fierce, stubborn, opposed to the established order and sure of themselves; and on the other are the bruised parents, anxious to make peace with their sons and daughters and meeting only rejection and contempt. The conflict was as old as the world, but particularly acute in the Russia of the 1860s. Dreamy-eyed liberalism was already giving way among the students to scientific materialism. To develop his ideological design in a novel, Turgenev needed a model. He found it, by his own admission, in August 1860, during a stay at

Ventnor on the Isle of Wight, where he had gone to bathe in the sea. "I must confess that I have never tried to create a type without having, not an idea, but a living person on which to base myself, one in whom all the various elements were harmoniously blended," he later wrote. "Not possessing to any very great degree the faculty of free invention, I have always needed some foundation in reality on which I could tread firmly. This was also the case for *Fathers and Sons;* the basis for Bazarov, the central character, was given to me by a striking personality, that of a young local doctor . . . This extraordinary man seemed to me to personify that principle which was then still in gestation but beginning to take form, and which was later given the name of nihilism. The impression this person made on me was at once powerful and indefinite. At first I could not define it to myself. But I observed and listened most closely to everything around me, as if to confirm the accuracy of my own sensations."[17]

He filled in his singular character's skeleton with features borrowed from young authors he had frequented in St. Petersburg, and the product of this spiritual fusion became the icy, rebellious Bazarov. A "new man," Bazarov acknowledges no religious, moral, or legal values and bows to scientific data alone. But unlike Rudin, for whom talking about a doctrine was enough, this man puts the doctrine into practice. He is contemptuous of comfort, cynical, and claims to be insensitive to the torments of the soul; so that is precisely where destiny strikes. He denies the reality of love and scorns tenderness, but he cannot resist the appeal of a woman. At the end of his struggle he is forced to admit that ideas are utterly powerless against the call of the heart, of blood. He dies stupidly, from an infected wound, and his parents mourn him without having understood him.

To define the philosophy of this tragic nay-sayer, Turgenev coined the term "nihilism." "A nihilist is a man who recognizes no authority," Bazarov's friend Arkady explains to his uncle, "a man who accepts no principle without first examining it, however high the esteem in which it may be held . . ." "Yes," the uncle answers, "in our day there were Hegelians, now they're nihilists. We shall see how you contrive to exist in emptiness, in the void, as though it were a vacuum machine. And now, my dear fellow, could you just touch the bell, I am feeling ready for my cocoa."

Nihilist Bazarov means to apply the rigorous methods of science to politics. He says he is tired of the old men's reformist verbiage. His elders' sins include, among others, that they waste their time talking, preach art for art's sake, support parliamentarianism and friendly settlements, and so on, instead of concerning themselves with people's daily bread. He sets himself up as the only realist in a generation of wet daydreamers. The elders, meanwhile, softly complain of being treated like useless dotards and nuisances by their hyperactive sons. "Our song is sung," they sigh. And yet they feel that there was a time when they too fought fervently for an ideal of justice. They remain loyal to their passion for art and poetry. They timidly try to get the young men to share their tastes, but the young men will have nothing to do with a literature that does not fight, is not effective, committed. All that matters to them is direct politics. They do not even condemn violence as a means to their ends.

In conceiving Bazarov, Turgenev achieved a tour de force, creating a type representative of the age and at the same time a believable human being. The author's talent transformed the doctrinaire into a man of flesh and blood. After closing the book, readers do not forget his presence, his obsession, something heavy and unforgettable in his character; he becomes a lifelong traveling companion. The other characters in the book are portrayed with the same resolute authority. With *Fathers and Sons* Turgenev shot far beyond his previous attainments and, in character analysis, descriptions of nature, and portrait of a social environment, reached a level of perfection that placed him foremost among the writers of his day.

Opinion was deeply stirred by the book, but both readers and critics were so preoccupied by the subject that they remained blind to its artistic value and saw only its political content. Turgenev had felt affection for his rebel-hero and had to fight back the tears when relating his death. "With the exception of his views on art, I share almost all Bazarov's other convictions," he said a few years later.[18] But for the conservatives, the character was a condemnation of the deviations of Russian youth, and they congratulated the author on the courage with which he had denounced the dangers of free thinking. The left-wing press, on the other hand, led by the *Contemporary,* was rabid. In that periodical a man named Antonovich criticized Turgenev's "outdated aestheticism," distorted presentation of progressive doctrines, contempt for the cause of women's emancipation, and shameless plundering of articles by Dobrolyubov to pad Bazarov's speeches. Young men saw the author of *Fathers and Sons* as a creature of reactionary blindness, an old-school master clutching his privileges, unable to understand the spirit of independence that was now sweeping over Russia. They turned away from him, insulted him at their meetings, burned his photographs. "I then observed a coldness akin

to hatred in people who had been close or well-disposed toward me,"
he wrote, "at the same time as I was being congratulated and almost
embraced by people in the opposing camp, by my enemies. I was
disconcerted and pained by all this. But my conscience was absolutely
clear. I knew that I had dealt honestly with the character I had tried
to portray and had drawn it not only without prejudice but positively
sympathetically."[19]

The Russian students in Heidelberg were made indignant by
Fathers and Sons, regarding it as a diatribe against their generation:
Turgenev answered them indirectly, in a letter to the poet Sluchevsky
who was with them at the time. His object, he said, was to make
people care for Bazarov, "with all his rough edges, coldheartedness,
and ruthless incisiveness." "I conceived him as a dark figure, wild and
huge, half-emerging from the clay, strong, unpleasant, honest, yet
doomed to perish because he still stands only on the threshold of the
future . . . And my young contemporaries are saying to me, 'You've
got it all wrong, mate, you have insulted us!' So all that is left for me,
as in the gypsy song, is to doff my cap and bow very low." In another
place, "My entire novel is directed against the nobility as a dominant
class. Take a good look at these characters [the fathers]. They reek of
feebleness, indolence, and narrowmindedness. My aesthetic sense led
me to choose good representatives of the aristocracy, the better to
prove my thesis. If the cream is bad, what must the milk be like?"[20]
But however he tried to justify himself, now humbly, now fiercely,
sometimes in face-to-face conversation and sometimes in letters to his
friends, a large proportion of his readers on the left felt that he had
betrayed their ideas. Dostoyevsky, Annenkov, Botkin, and Tyuchev
were singing his praises, but Fet, Aksakov, even Herzen condemned
him for writing a sort of propaganda, too visibly aimed at the new men
on the *Contemporary.* His detractors glibly forgot his defense of persecuted revolutionaries. At the beginning of the year, in Paris, he had
given a roof to Bakunin, who had escaped from Siberia, provided him
with an annual stipend of five thousand francs, and launched a fund
on his behalf. Back in St. Petersburg, he had asked for and obtained
permission to visit Bakunin's brothers who were imprisoned in Sts.
Peter and Paul Fortress. These acts, added to his open friendship with
Herzen, made the authorities suspicious of him—but they were not
enough to whiten him in the eyes of the progressives. Bazarov's name
was written across his breast like a placard of infamy. Whatever he did
and whatever he said, henceforth he stood convicted of the crime of
lèse- youth.

8

BADEN-BADEN

For some time Pauline Viardot had been aware that her powerful, warm contralto voice was weakening. At every performance she was afraid her vocal chords would give way. In her latest triumph, Gluck's *Orphée,* she was already acting more than singing. So, rather than submit to the indifference of an audience that had once adored her, she decided to retire. She was forty-one, she still had her presence, her fiery gaze, and her captivating smile. Surrounded by her four children (Louise, the eldest; Claudie, or Didie as she was called, who was Turgenev's favorite; Marianne; and the four-year-old Paul), she determined to live a quiet life. She would teach, organize concerts, write music. She might perfectly well have settled in Paris, but she hated the thought of living in retirement in a place where she used to be the toast of the town and, like her husband and Turgenev, she was opposed to the authoritarian government of Napoleon III.

After selling the château of Courtavenel, she moved to Baden-Baden in Germany, living first in a rented apartment and then in a large villa that she bought, intending it as a permanent home. Turgenev's gaze immediately turned toward the quiet, green watering place that now sheltered the woman he had never ceased to love. In Russia, the hostility of one part of his fellow citizens toward himself and his work was a painful ordeal. Overexcited striplings were positively driving him out of his homeland: Why shouldn't he take a little trip to Germany, for a change of air? To Baden-Baden he duly went, and was charmed by its rural aspect and by Pauline Viardot's reception of him. After a lengthy cooling-off period in their relations, he now found her as vivacious, alluring, and well disposed as in the balmiest days of their union. It wasn't love that she felt, no, but a tender friendship, a fraternal esteem that filled his aching heart like the soft warmth of a sunset.

In this idyllic atmosphere he read Herzen's first articles in the *Bell* titled "Ends and Beginnings," written in the form of open letters to himself. Although he admired Herzen's generous ideals, Turgenev could no longer follow his friend's new pan-Slavist tendencies; the publicist was attacking the petty, money-grubbing civilization of western Europe and glorifying the ancestral values of the Russian people— the only people, according to him, who were capable of saving mankind from total collapse. Bakunin and Ogarev had allied themselves with Herzen. Russia's mission as reviver of the race seemed self-evident to them, and they were energetically demolishing anyone who, like Turgenev, still believed in the improving virtues of the West. They accused him of drifting away from them out of weakness and idleness, "epicureanism," or possibly old age. Cut to the quick, Turgenev wrote back to Herzen that his attachment to Western principles and institutions was very definitely not a symptom of senility: "Were I twenty years old I should do the same, not out of personal interest but in the interest of the people."[1] He sat down to compose a reply to the articles in the *Bell,* but asked Herzen to publish it anonymously in order to escape prosecution. Before he even finished writing it, however, he was given official warning by the Russian authorities, forbidding him to contribute in any way to such a seditious publication. He prudently refrained from compromising himself further and simply showed Herzen the pages he had already written. He also refused to sign an "address to Alexander II" written by Ogarev, with the approval of Herzen and Bakunin, about the peasants' new status. He saw it as a maneuver that was more likely to backfire than not and a dreadful distortion of democratic ideas. "The gist of my disagreement with Ogarev, Herzen, and Bakunin lies in the fact that they spurn the educated class of Russia and drag it through the mud, and they allege that the revolution or reforms will come from the people," he wrote to Longinin. "But in reality the revolution, in the keenest and broadest sense of the word, will come from the minority of that same educated class, and that will be enough to carry it to victory, if we do not exterminate ourselves in the meantime."[2] Again, in a letter to Herzen, "I cannot give my support to Ogarev, firstly because he is putting forward the old socialist theories of collective ownership and I do not agree with them, and secondly because, in the matter of the freeing of the serfs, he shows complete failure to understand the life of the people and the needs of the moment."[3] Despite his differences with Turgenev, Bakunin was grateful for his efforts to persuade the authorities to release his wife, who was still being held in Siberia, and allow her to join him. "You are one of the few in the opposing camp to have remained our friend," he wrote, "and with you alone we can talk heart to heart."[4] But to Longinin Bakunin wrote what he really thought: "Turgenev is a gifted writer and a charming man, but in politics he's a buffoon."[5]

Spurned by his Russian friends, Turgenev drew closer to the Viardot clan. Pauline, her husband, and their children were his family, almost his spiritual homeland. In the spring of 1863 he rented an apartment in Baden-Baden and moved into it with his daughter and Mrs. Innis, the governess. Since Pauline had chosen to live there, the little German burg had become a second Courtavenel; for Turgenev, the entire landscape was permeated with her feminine presence. There were walks along the paths in the park, sparkling conversations with guests, music recitals or readings, and, intermittently, work on the short story "Phantoms," which he had promised Dostoyevsky long ago. These multiple activities gave Turgenev a rare sense of plenitude. For him, Louis Viardot was more than a pleasant fellow to talk to and a jolly hunting companion; he was a sensitive and knowledgeable man with a passion for literature. Together, he and Turgenev translated works by Gogol and Pushkin into French, along with a few of his own writings. He respected and was fond of Viardot, although he did not share all his views about art. He had now reached some sort of ambivalent comfort between husband and wife, a dissembling peace that took the place of happiness for him. But even in Baden-Baden he could not shake off all his cares. At the end of the previous year a messenger from Herzen had been arrested at the Austro-Italian frontier, bearing banned books and letters from the émigrés in London to their supporters in Russia. Turgenev's name cropped up again and again in their correspondence, and on orders from the government he was implicated in the trial of the "London propagandists," also known as the "Case of the Thirty-two." Summoned to appear before a committee of senators in St. Petersburg and give an account of his association with revolutionary circles, he took the advice of Budberg, the Russian ambassador in Paris, and wrote directly to the emperor protesting his innocence: "I am a writer, Your Majesty, and nothing more. My entire life is expressed in my works and it is on them that I must be judged. I dare hope that anyone who will take the trouble to consider them attentively will agree, in all fairness, that my convictions, which are both independent and sincere, are very moderate indeed."[6] And as a matter of fact, it was rather silly to condemn him for being friendly with the political exiles, when they were rejecting him as an obsolete liberal. "That I should be summoned to appear before the Senate now," he wrote to Annenkov, "after *Fathers and Sons,* after the insulting reviews of the younger generation and after a final and almost public break with the outlaws in London, or rather with their way of thinking, remains quite totally incomprehensible to me."[7]

In reality, Turgenev had always been a misfit in every aspect of his life. He was close to the extremist conspirators, but not a revolutionary; he was Russian to the very soles of his feet, but happy only abroad; he had been in love with the same woman for twenty years and lived beside her without hope of anything more than a kind word. Pulled by two ideas, two countries, and two destinies, he suffered from constant inner conflict, yet at the same time it gave him a kind of mournful satisfaction. In his letter to the emperor he gave ill health as his reason for not returning to Russia and asked, as a special favor, to be sent a questionnaire that would enable him to explain his position. The moment he received the document he sat down to complete it, sincerely and astutely, point by point. It emerged from his explanation that he had become friendly with Bakunin and Herzen in his youth, before the two men had become revolutionaries, and that he had continued to be fond of them thereafter but that for many years he had ceased to share their political views. Herzen, unintentionally bearing him out, printed a calumnious anecdote in the *Bell,* affirming that the author of *Fathers and Sons* had made light of the Russian army's alleged exactions in Poland. Turgenev indignantly wrote demanding that he retract the item: "I am deeply offended by this mud that has been thrown on my solitary, virtually secret life." He added, "Our views differ too widely. What is the point of continuing to goad each other? I do not propose that we prolong our correspondence."

Despite his professions of loyalty the Senate commission was not satisfied and sent him a fresh summons in connection with the "Case of the Thirty-two." If he did not comply with it, his possessions in Russia were in danger of confiscation. No further procrastination was possible. In Baden-Baden, meanwhile, skies were gray. Paulinette had quarreled with Pauline Viardot, so Turgenev sent her back to Paris and asked a friend, Madame Delessert, a woman much in view in literary circles, to find her a husband posthaste. Then he set out.

What worried him most was not what was awaiting him in St. Petersburg but what he was leaving behind in Baden-Baden. He felt as if he were being forcibly torn from his rightful place. As soon as he reached Berlin he wrote to Pauline Viardot: "It is a quarter past seven in the evening, dear Madame Viardot. At this moment you are all gathered in the drawing room. You are playing music, Viardot is nodding by the fire, the children are drawing, and I, whose heart is also in your beloved drawing room, am preparing to sleep a little more . . . I see myself as a man dreaming, I cannot get used to the idea that I am already so far from Baden, and people and things move past before my eyes without seeming to touch me."[8] Upon reaching his destination, he wrote again: "Baden? Alas, no! St. Petersburg, Monday, January 6/18, 1864. Dear good Madame Viardot, My hand, in writing the treasured name of Baden at the top of the page, has betrayed my constant thoughts. But I am all too certainly in St. Petersburg!"[9]

The next day he went to the Senate and was ushered into a huge room in which sat six elderly gentlemen wearing uniforms paved with decorations. "I was kept standing for an hour," he related. "The answers I had sent them were read out to me, I was asked if I had anything further to add to them, then I was sent away and told to come back Monday to be interviewed at the same time as another man. Everybody was very courteous, very quiet, which is an excellent sign." At the following session he was required to provide further particulars, in writing, in a record book. There was no "hearing" in the presence of any other "party." The faces of the members of the commission were affable; they plainly thought they were dealing not with a disrupter of the peace but with a great writer who stood high in His Majesty's graces. "I wasn't even interrogated," Turgenev wrote to Pauline Viardot. "My six judges seemed to prefer to chat with me about nothing in particular."[10] At last, on January 28, 1864, he was given permission to leave the country again. In the *Bell,* Herzen immediately ascribed the judges' leniency to the ignoble obsequiousness of the accused. His article referred to a "graying Magdalen (of masculine sex) who had written to the tsar to inform him that her appetite was failing, she could not sleep, she had lost a few gray hairs and one or two teeth and was wringing her hands in anguish because the emperor hadn't yet heard how terribly penitent she was and how, as a result, she had broken off all relations with the friends of her youth."[11]

Informed of this new piece of nastiness, Turgenev wrote to Herzen a few weeks later: "That Bakunin, having borrowed money from me and thoughtlessly put me in a most unpleasant position by his malicious gossip, should have strewed muck about me on every side is only part of the natural order of things and, knowing him as long as I have, I expected no more from him. But I could hardly presume that you, like him, would be flinging filth at a man who had been close to you for twenty years, simply because he no longer held exactly the same opinions as you. If I had been able to show you my replies to the questionnaire you would almost certainly be convinced that without hiding anything I not only avoided giving offense to any of my friends but did not even try to impugn them, which I would have considered unworthy of me. I confess that I am rather proud when I think of those replies."[12]

To forget the spitefulness of his former émigré friends, he plunged headling into the social life of the capital. There were dinners with Annenkov and Botkin, melancholic visits to his dear Countess Lambert, now more pious than ever; there were evenings at the opera, concerts conducted by Rubenstein, a meeting of the committee for the welfare of needy writers, a reception at the Italian embassy, a ball at the Assembly of Nobility that was attended by the emperor. "I saw the tsar," he wrote to Pauline Viardot, "and to my mind he is a fine figure of a man."[13] He also attended literary banquets at which he spoke of his relations with Western writers, found a publisher for some love songs composed by Pauline Viardot, was reconciled with Goncharov and saw the publication of his story "Phantoms" in Dostoyevsky's new periodical, *Epoch,* its predecessor *(Time)* having been barred by the authorities. The story is distinctly fantastic in tone and reflects a philosophy that shows signs of heavy borrowing from Schopenhauer. There is the sublime indifference of nature, the futility of human activity, the frailty and vanity of works of art, the sense of self-loathing. The idea of flying birdlike through the stratosphere had pursued him since that dream of levitation he had recounted to Pauline Viardot in 1849. "I felt so weary of everything," says the narrator in "Phantoms," "more than weary. I no longer even felt pity for my brethren. All my feelings merged into one, to which I hardly dare give a name: a feeling of loathing and, stronger than all the rest, there was within me a loathing of myself." Friends and critics were disconcerted by this mixture of unreality and bitter pessimism. In the *Contemporary* Antonovich said the story was strung together out of bits and pieces and left an indefinable impression upon the reader. A young critic, Pisarev, in *Russian Work,* spoke of "futility," while others suggested that the tale was an inferior piece written long ago and left moldering in a drawer, or that the springs of the author's talent had dried up. As for Dostoyevsky, after complimenting Turgenev hypocritically and saying how delighted he was to publish the story in the first issue of *Epoch,* he wrote to his brother Michael, "In my opinion it is full of excrement, there is something unclean, unhealthy, senile in it, something weak and therefore unbelievable, in a word it's pure Turgenev, with all his convictions, but the poetry will make up for much."[14] Turgenev, meanwhile, was telling Pauline Viardot, "My friends are a little frightened, and murmur about it being 'absurd.' "[15]

For some time he had been feeling that there was nothing more for him to do in Russia. "It is impossible for me to tell you how continually I think of you," he wrote, once again, to Pauline Viardot. "My heart literally melts with affection the moment your dear image—I shall not say arises in my thoughts because it is never out of them—but seems to draw a little closer."[16] At the end of February he returned to Baden-Baden and from there to Paris, to embrace his daughter, on whose behalf Madame Delessert was actively matchmaking. Paulinette had just refused her hand to one M. Pinet. "I have never wished anything but a marriage of affection for you," her father told her, "and should that element be lacking the rest is nothing. So there is one more suitor gone, let us hear no more of him."[17]

Thereupon he learned that in Petersburg the trial of the "Thirty-two" had ended and that he himself had been completely cleared, while people guilty of very little more than himself had been given heavy sentences. Some suspects had even been sent to the hard labor camps in Siberia. Turgenev was glad to get off so lightly, but it made him uneasy to think that other people had been less favored than he. From then on, his break with the London exiles was complete. He minded, because he liked people to like him. Work was the only thing that could relieve his discomfort. While staying with Paulinette and her governess, he wrote a short story, "The Dog," in two days and started on a "Homage to Shakespeare." After that, he headed back to Baden-Baden, drawn by the irresistible Pauline Viardot. But it was not only herself he wanted to see: it was the family too, the husband and children. Away from them he was not himself, he felt he was wasting his time. It occurred to him that he might establish himself permanently somewhere close by. He bought a piece of land near the Viardots' villa and decided to build on it a Louis XIII–style house to be designed by a French architect, complete with turrets, slate roof, broad, airy rooms, a theater, glass doors, and a semicircular terrace. It was to take three years to complete, and the estimated cost was considerable—fifty thousand francs. To pay for it, Turgenev instructed his uncle Nicholas Turgenev, who was managing his estate at Spasskoye, to sell land as fast as he could and at any price. He was sacrificing his Russian roots to his love for Pauline Viardot, cheerfully abandoning the fields and forests in which he had dreamed away his childhood and youth, gun in hand, to build himself a "nest" in Germany. To Countess Lambert, who accused him of neglecting his homeland, he retorted, "It is in no sense indispensable for a writer to live in his homeland and try to apprehend every transformation that takes place there. In any event, it is not indispensable that he be there all the time . . . In short, I see no reason why I should not settle in Baden. I do it not out of any desire for pleasure (that is something for young people), but simply to weave myself a nest in which I can await the inevitable end."[18] Countess Lambert also reproached him for not being a good Orthodox churchgoer, and on this point he agreed. "I am not a Christian as you understand the term, and probably I am not one in any sense."[19]

But although he called himself a freethinker, he had a strong sense of family tradition and bourgeois respectability. He rejoiced to learn that, thanks to the efforts of Madame Delessert, Paulinette had finally found a fiancé to her liking, one Gaston Bruère, a glass manufacturer from Rougemont. Turgenev applied to the Viardots for help in amassing the sum required for her dowry, and they advanced the necessary funds. Then he went to Paris for the wedding preparations. "I am boiling here [in Paris], it's like a stewpot," he wrote to Annenkov. "The notaries are squeezing me to the last drop, and what makes it worse is that my future son-in-law was once a notary himself."[20]

The wedding was on February 25, 1865. That same day, after the ceremony, Turgenev returned to Baden-Baden to supervise work on his house. It was costing far more than he had anticipated. On several occasions he had to borrow in order to pay the bills. These financial worries interfered with his work, but he managed to produce one short story, "Enough!" and send it to St. Petersburg. It was even bleaker than "Phantoms"; the readers disliked it and the critics were indignant. The *Book Messenger* said the author was unfeeling, deplored his hopeless languor, and advised him to retire from the literary scene.

Later, in the *Work,* Shelgunov wrote, "Since the abolition of serfdom Turgenev is dead and has ceased to serve the cause he swore to defend at eighteen."

With his readers sulking and the journalists sharpening their claws on him, Turgenev felt as if he had outlived his reputation, for better or for worse. Even so, he found strength to start another big novel, *Smoke.* He worked at it slowly, intermittently. His correspondence with his Russian friends in St. Petersburg and Moscow took up a great deal of his time. Some of them came to visit him in Baden-Baden—among them Annenkov, Botkin, Goncharov. And, of course, he kept up with everything that was being published in Russia. His judgments were severe. Tolstoy's *1805,* the first part of *War and Peace,* was a disappointment. "To me this is a truly bad, boring failure of a novel."[21] Nor did he find anything to like in Dostoyevsky's *Crime and Punishment.* "It is something in the manner of a colic prolonged by an epidemic of cholera. God preserve us!"[22]

And yet, even though he was so short of money himself, Turgenev sent fifty German thalers to the very same Dostoyevsky, who had lost his shirt gambling in Wiesbaden and came crying to him for help.

For the most part, he felt a stranger to the violence and disorder and insanity he saw in some of his fellow countrymen. He was appalled to learn of the attempted assassination of the tsar on April 4, 1866, by a man named Karakozov. The sovereign's escape was almost miraculous: a simple peasant named Komisarov had as if instinctively struck the assassin's hand aside. The emotion this aroused in Russia verged upon mass hysteria. Russians abroad too, were expostulating, wondering, having premonitions of tragic aftermaths. Along with the other Russians in Baden-Baden, Turgenev attended a thanksgiving mass. "This time there was no discord," he wrote to Annenkov. "Every emotion blended into one. I shudder to think what would have become of Russia had this crime been accomplished."[23] Six days later he asked Annenkov to send him a photograph of the man who had deflected the shot intended for the tsar, and added that he approved of the congratulatory message addressed to the sovereign by the committee for the welfare of needy writers. "It is essential, not for us but for many ill-intentioned persons, that the horror inspired by the indescribable act of that person whom I absolutely cannot regard as a Russian should be given full voice by the literary world," he wrote.[24]

The crisis subsided, he resumed his habitual divertissements.

Pauline had formed a music center in Baden-Baden. She was giving singing lessons to young people of good family and directing operettas that she had composed. Turgenev, neglecting his big novel, cheerfully complied with his beloved's every whim and dashed off facile libretti for her—*Le Dernier des sorciers, L'Ogre, Trop de femmes* [*The Last of the Witches, The Ogre, Too Many Wives*]. The company was composed of the pupils of the mistress of the house. Now and then Turgenev himself took a part. All this froth and flutter made him feel like a young man again. He gesticulated, made people laugh, was applauded for something other than his books. The audience on these occasions was formed of the very cream of the local elite. Sometimes the King and Queen of Prussia were there, or the Grand Duke and Grand Duchess of Baden, princes and princesses, noted foreigners.

When Turgenev's house was finally finished, he didn't have enough money left to furnish it, so it stood empty until more funds arrived from Russia. Once he was settled in, the performances were transferred there, to the theater he had planned for Pauline's joy and grandeur. His feelings for her now were steadfastly loving. He was sorry to leave her, in February, for a trip to Russia, where his uncle Nicholas was, it seemed to him, making a sorry muddle of the management of his estate.

Once there, he entrusted the administration of Spasskoye to a steward named Kishinsky, which so infuriated Uncle Nicholas that he shut himself up in his bedroom and began issuing "insane" missives to him through a servant. In his baggage Turgenev had brought the manuscript of *Smoke* and two short stories, "Lieutenant Yurgunov" and "The Brigadier." In St. Petersburg, and then in Moscow, he read his latest works to a few friends, who heartily applauded them. But were those friends sincere? His previous books had taken such a drubbing in the press that he was afraid to publish anything new. On the other hand, he needed money. To put his finances on an even keel again, he was going to have to "flog my muse for the next two years," he said, "and count myself lucky at that because literature pays."[25]

On April 4, 1867, he set out for Baden-Baden, feeling that he was returning to his adopted home. Eight days later the *Russian Messenger* published *Smoke*. Turgenev was not displeased to be out of Russia just then—distance, he thought, might soften his enemies' blows.

Varvara Petrovna, mother of Turgenev.
Photo D. R.

Sergey Nikolayevich, father of Turgenev.
Photo D. R.

Turgenev in 1830, at the age of twelve. *Photo Flammarion*

Turgenev in 1846. *Photo D. R.*

Turgenev. Drawing by A. A. Bakunin. *Photo D. R.*

Turgenev. Drawing by Pauline Viardot. *Photo D. R.*

Dostoyevsky. 1881
photograph. *Photo Novosty Press
Agency*

Photograph of young Tolstoy.
Photo Bibliothèque Nationale

Pauline Viardot at the piano. Photographed in Berlin, 1860. *Photo Bibliothèque Nationale*

Pauline Viardot. *Photo Novosty Press Agency*

Louis Viardot. Taken from *l'Illustration*, September 29, 1883. *Photo Flammarion*

Pauline Viardot's Parisian salon. Engraving shown in *Tableau de Paris*, by Texier, in 1852. From the Library of Ornamental Arts, Paris. *Photo Jean-Loup Charmet*

Paulinette Bruère, Turgenev's daughter, in a photograph taken in 1870. *Photo D. R.*

Flaubert, in a photograph by Nadar. *Photo Bibliothèque Nationale*

Page from a Turgenev manuscript: *On the Eve. Photo Flammarion*

Saint Petersburg in the nineteenth century: the Nevsky Prospect; to the left, the City Council. From the Museum of History, Moscow. *Photo Novosty Press Agency*

The Spasskoye House. From the Turgenev Library, Paris. *Photo D. R.*

The château of Courtavenel. *Photo Flammarion*

Turgenev's villa at Baden-Baden. *Photo D. R.*

The Viardots' villa at Bougival. Taken from *Bougival et les rives de la Seine* by M. and E. Houth. *Photo Diguet-Deny, 1970*

Turgenev's chalet at Bougival. *Photo D. R.*

Turgenev. Portrait by Pauline Viardot circa 1878. *Photo Roger-Viollet*

Turgenev's bedroom in his chalet at Bougival (re-created by the Boulle School). *Photo Ville de La Celle-Saint-Cloud*

Turgenev hunting. 1879 portrait. *Photo D. R.*

Turgenev, self-portrait. *Photo Flammarion*

Turgenev wearing the cape of Oxford University's *honoris causa*. *Photo Novosty Press Agency*

Turgenev at his home at Spasskoye. Painting by Chtcherbakov. *Photo Novosty Press Agency*

Turgenev. *Photo Roger-Viollet*

Turgenev ill, in his bedroom at Bougival. Drawing by Claudia Chamerot, 1883. *Photo Flammarion*

Turgenev on his deathbed. *Photo Jean-Loup Charmet*

Funeral procession for Turgenev in St. Petersburg, 1883. *Photo D. R.*

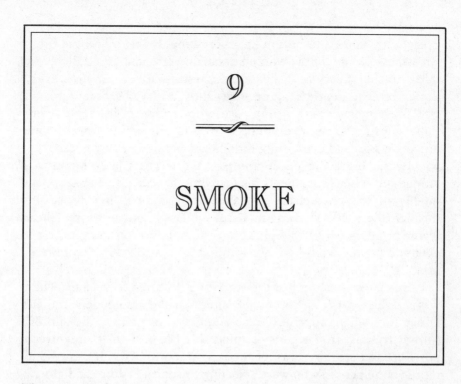

9

SMOKE

The source of the love story in *Smoke* is the same as that in *A Nest of Gentlefolk*. Litvinov, the hero of the new novel, is another hesitant, ambivalent Hamlet. He is staying in Baden-Baden with his fiancée, the gentle Tatyana, and her aunt Capitolina Shestov. While there, he meets by chance a beautiful, intense, and capricious young woman named Irena with whom he had once been so deeply in love that he had wanted to marry her; but Irena, after making rather a splash on her first appearance in society, had abandoned him for a more glittering fate. She and her husband, an affable, elegant, self-satisfied general, now presided over the little Russian circle in town. After seeing Litvinov again, her one idea is to reconquer him; and he, without putting up even a semblance of a fight, surrenders. He knows full well that this second love for the wild and fickle Irena will lead to his destruction but nevertheless breaks off his engagement to his fiancée and asks Irena to elope with him. At the last moment, after ruining his life a second time, she decides not to run away with him but to stay with her husband. In the train taking him back to Russia, Litvinov, "numb" with grief, stares at the smoke from the locomotive, which the wind is driving back down onto the station platform. "He was alone in the compartment," Turgenev wrote. "There was no one to disturb him. 'Smoke, smoke,' he repeated several times; suddenly

89

everything seemed to be smoke, everything, his own life, the life of Russia, everything in the whole human universe and especially everything Russian. Everything, he thought, is just smoke and vapor; everything seems to keep changing incessantly, everywhere new images, new phenomena, are thrusting each other aside; yet in reality everything stays the same; everything is rushing, hastening toward some unknown goal and everything disappears without leaving a trace, and without having achieved anything." A few years later Litvinov, a sadder and wiser man, meets his erstwhile fiancée Tatyana again and quietly marries her. Irena, meanwhile, continues her procession through the social firmament. Rich, adulated, and unhappy, she is feared by all the "best" people because of her position and power, and even the young avoid her, not wanting to confront her "embittered mind."

But *Smoke* was not just the story of a thwarted love affair. There was a double satire in the novel, aimed at the resplendent military nonentities who comprise Irena's entourage and also at the author's former friends. In Turgenev's mind this book, with its mixture of nostalgia and acerbity, was meant as a direct reply to Herzen and all those young people who were rejecting European culture and glorifying Slavic mysticism. Heckled and badgered by them, he was retorting with a degree of irony and vehemence that bore witness to his unflagging vitality. It is true that physically he was no daredevil, but his beautiful manners and his pliancy did not prevent him from braving insult, enmity, and discredit in order to stand by his convictions. Battles of ideas did not scare him; sometimes he even went in search of them. In *Smoke,* a character named Potugin inveighs against the people who are criticizing him for showing too great an attachment to foreign countries: "I love and hate my Russia," he said, "my strange, adorable, abominable and dear homeland. Now I have left it; I needed a bit of air . . . I have left Russia and I find it very pleasant to be here; but I shall soon go back, I feel it . . ." Elsewhere the same character rails against Russian art, Russian arrogance, and Russian backwardness in all things. Turgenev would certainly not have approved all of Potugin's ideas, but his love of the West made him at least partly his character's accomplice. Even when he was proclaiming himself quintessentially Russian, a sort of European aura floated around him.

He expected reaction to his book in Russia to be strong, but it far exceeded his direst fears. Conservative circles were outraged by his jaundiced portrayal of high society, Slavophiles took him to task for denigrating his native land, revolutionaries called him a senile dodderer incapable of understanding the value of the young Russian strength. Herzen, to whom he had sent a copy of the novel, hailed it in the *Bell* with venom: "Poor old Ivan Sergeyevich [Turgenev] didn't really need to go blowing smoke rings like these! After all, nature has endowed him with so many abilities: he knows how to talk about hunting, he knows how to shoot down, with his pen, all manner of capercaillies and partridges living in 'master's nests' and 'ends of the earth.' But no, says he, I want to be a caustic, nasty, bilious commentator on public affairs, when in reality there is not one drop of nastiness or bile in the man's whole warm heart . . ." And to Turgenev he wrote, "I frankly own that Potugin bores me. Why didn't you leave out at least half of his verbiage?" Stung, Turgenev replied, "Potugin bores you and you're sorry I didn't leave out at least half of his speeches. How odd; because I personally find that he still doesn't say enough, and the universal furor which this character has unleashed against me makes me think I must be right."[1] To Pisarev, the young critic, he similarly affirmed, "The character may be beloved of myself alone, but I am glad that he exists and that people are firing red-hot bullets at him in the thick of the pan-Slavist intoxication now reigning in Russia. I am glad that at this precise moment I was able to run the flag of 'civilization' up my flagpole. Let them throw mud on it from all sides, if that's what they like."[2] The government press accused Turgenev of "offending national feeling," being a "liar" and "calumniator" and ignorant of all things Russian. "I know the whole world is calling me names," Turgenev wrote again, to Herzen, "red and white, from above and below and from the side—especially from the side. Indignant verses have even been published. But that does not bother me."[3] Some critics thought the polemics detracted from the love story of Litvinov and Irena. Others said that the author had run out of steam and his latest novel was a throwback to the aesthetics of the 1840s.

One of the most fervent demolishers of *Smoke* was Dostoyevsky. He had long cherished a pathological antagonism to Turgenev. He could not tolerate the languid aristocrat's smooth gentility, his courteous condescension. *Smoke* hurt his patriotism. But he had not forgotten that he owed its author fifty thalers. On a visit to Baden-Baden, encouraged by his wife, he decided to visit Turgenev. Not in order to pay off his debt—the roulette table had ruined him permanently—but in order to tell him that he meant to pay it off some day. Tempers flared from the very start of the interview. "He told me he was a complete atheist," Dostoyevsky wrote to his friend Maykov. "But good God, deism gave us Christ, I mean, so lofty a representation of man that it is impossible to understand him without worshipping him and to doubt that he is mankind's eternal ideal. And what have they given us, all these Turgenevs and Herzens and Utins and Chernyshevskys? . . . They're all so shamefully irritable, so stupidly conceited, it doesn't seem true. What do they hope for? And who will follow them?" What infuriated Dostoyevsky most, he said, was Turgenev's open display of contempt for Russia. "Among other things, he told me that we should crawl to the Germans because there was only one way, ineluctable and common to all, and that way was civilization; and that all specific and original Russian initiatives were uncouth and stupid. He also told me that he was writing a long article on Russophiles and Slavophiles. Then I said that he should have a telescope sent out from Paris, it would make his task easier. 'Why?' he asked. 'Because you're in a good viewing position here,' I told him, 'to point your telescope at Russia and examine us; otherwise, you'd hardly be able to see us.' That made him angry. When I saw that he was well and truly in a temper I went on, 'I hadn't supposed that the poor response to *Smoke* and all those nasty articles could upset you as much as that. I assure you, it isn't worth it. Don't think about them.' 'What's got into you?' he snapped, scarlet with anger and embarrassment. 'I'm not in the least upset!' " Dostoyevsky added, "I can't take any more of him. He has insulted me too deeply with his notions . . . One really cannot listen to Russia being treated to such insults by a Russian traitor who might have made himself useful. I had already remarked, four years ago, upon his way of crawling to the Germans and his dislike of Russians. But his present positively rabid irritation with and persecution of Russia come solely from the failure of *Smoke*, and the fact that Russia has dared not to claim him as a genius. There's nothing but personal vanity in it, and that only makes it all the more revolting."[4]

The two men parted on bad terms. Dostoyevsky went home delighted to have goaded the rootless aristocrat into a rage. His representation of Turgenev's anti-Russian statements, in the account he gave Maykov, was no doubt grossly exaggerated. But there is also no doubt that Dostoyevsky's obstinately Slavophile, Orthodox, messianic attitudes grated on Turgenev and that he yielded to the temptation to contradict him on every possible occasion. In any event, the publicity given in Russia to his letter to Maykov was unfortunate. Maykov himself copied out some passages and transmitted them to Bartenyev, editor of the *Russian Archives,* with the suggestion that he "preserve the document for posterity." Turgenev, forewarned by Annenkov, wrote Bartenyev a letter of protest: "I feel bound to say that I should have thought it very much out of place to express my intimate convictions [about Russia and Russians] in front of Mr. Dostoyevsky, if only because I regard him as a man who, owing to his bouts of illness, and for other reasons, is not in perfect possession of his faculties. This opinion is shared by many persons, moreover. I saw Mr. Dostoyevsky only once; he spent no more than an hour with me and, after relieving himself by cruelly insulting the German people, myself, and my book, he left. I had neither time nor inclination to make objections. I tell you, I treated him as a sick man. The arguments he thought he heard coming from me presumably presented themselves to his own fevered imagination, so that he wrote this report for posterity against me. It is likely that in 1890 neither Mr. Dostoyevsky nor myself will be commanding the attention of our fellow countrymen. But if we have not been utterly forgotten, we shall be judged not on biased hearsay but on the result of a whole life and a whole work."[5]

Not even Turgenev's close friends could agree with his indictment of the "Russian spirit" as it appeared in the characters in *Smoke.* Dear old Fet, the companion of so many hunting parties, conversations, and daydreams, wrote to Tolstoy, "Have you read the famous novel *Smoke?* . . . It consists of insults to all things Russian, at the very moment when everyone in Russia is doing their utmost to be Russian . . . According to him, everything in Russia is hateful and stupid and must be shaken up and overturned and done again, in the foreign manner."[6] Tolstoy, not displeased to see a colleague in the soup, replied, "I have long wanted to write to you about *Smoke* and, naturally, tell you exactly what you tell me . . . As regards *Smoke,* I think that the force of poetry is in love; the direction taken by that force depends upon character. Without the force of love there is no poetry . . . In *Smoke* there is love for nothing, or almost nothing, and so there is almost no poetry. The only love is for a superficial, trifling adulterer and that is why the poetry in this novel is objectionable."[7] The Russians in Germany were also giving the author a hard time. "Since the publication of *Smoke,*" Turgenev wrote to Borisov, "the Russian nabobs here have stopped asking me to their shooting parties."[8]

Despite the mountain of criticism piling up around him, Turgenev stood his ground. "There is nothing surprising in the fact that you disliked *Smoke,*" he wrote to Fet. "I should have been surprised by any other reaction. Besides, there is almost nobody who likes the book. And, would you believe it, I couldn't care less and would not give a farthing for your approval. Believe it or not, I am sure this book is the only relevant and useful thing I have written."9

He even thought of composing a preface to the novel, reaffirming his European allegiance: "I should demonstrate even more forcefully the need for us Russians to continue taking lessons from the Germans, just as the Germans took lessons from the Romans, etc."10

In reality, this much-maligned novel was at once a solid, bold, and melancholic piece of work. The descriptions of characters and settings in it have a photographic precision. The discussions of political and artistic issues are skillfully interwoven with the twists and turns of the plot. At the end, the readers are left with a complex sense of nostalgia, apprehension, and pessimism. They too are as if shrouded in smoke. Turgenev was not wrong when he claimed that this was one of the best books he had written.

Contemplating the onslaught being made upon him, he felt that he was more appreciated, better loved abroad than at home. Moscow and St. Petersburg were tearing him to shreds, but in France, England, Germany, his books were being translated; he was being praised in Parisian literary circles. He belonged to two worlds, in truth: one was the world of the young progressive Slavophile writers, the poisonous articles in the periodicals, the sour discussions with Uncle Nicholas, the money worries resulting from a poorly managed estate; the other was the world of his adoration of Pauline Viardot, the daily alms of her gaze and voice, shooting with the husband, Germanic placidity and cleanliness, the green hills, a cosmopolitan, wealthy, pasteurized atmosphere, a paradise for gouty, moonsick bachelors. How could he be expected to give up his European haven for a bear pit in Russia? Was it his fault if he was a double man, neither all revolutionary nor all conservative, neither all Russian nor all foreign, not quite lover and not quite friend? His fellow countrymen didn't know what label to put on him and were exasperated by their inability to do so; they interpreted his duality as a betrayal of their native land by one of its greatest authors. He alone knew that he was never more Russian than when he was writing, pen in hand, beyond the frontiers of his own country.

He was deeply shocked when he heard that Tsar Alexander II had been the victim of another assassination attempt, on May 6, 1867, during a visit to Paris. By chance the bullet had gone wide and the man with the gun, a young Polish refugee, was arrested on the spot. To Turgenev these repeated efforts to murder an enlightened sovereign were the product of mindless fanaticism. On May 31 he made a point of accompanying other Russian expatriates to the Baden-Baden railway station to salute the emperor on his return to Russia. "The emperor came through here today," he announced to his friend the writer Pisemsky, "and we all went to meet him at the station. It seemed to me that he had lost much weight. But how unspeakably vile, that Polono-Parisian gunshot!"[11]

A few days later he went to Paris himself to see his daughter, Paulinette, and visit the World's Fair with her. The Russian pavilion disappointed him. "But," he wrote to Annenkov, "I shall say nothing about it because people would start howling again about how unpatriotic I am." Otherwise, he said, he was tremendously impressed by the scope and quality of this manifestation of friendship between peoples: "What I feel about this exhibition is exuberant admiration; it is indisputably a unique and astonishing thing . . . In its way, a masterpiece."[12] Decidedly, the times when he felt most at home were when he could embrace all the civilizations of the globe in a single glance.

Both that year and the next, however, he went to Russia several times, to see friends, sell land, and renew his contact with the countryside. His peasants were a disappointment. "Freedom has not made them richer; on the contrary,"[13] he wrote to Pauline Viardot. At the other extreme of the social ladder, his relations with literary circles became even more strained than before. "I see perfectly well that my extended stays abroad have an adverse effect on my literary activity and may destroy it completely," he told Polonsky. "But nothing can be done about it."[14] And later, to the poet Zhemchuzhnikov, "It is not easy to say in words how deeply the present generation dislikes me. At every step, whether I will or no, I come up against expressions of hatred, even contempt."[15]

This systematic denigration did not incline him to humility, however; far from it. He did not easily bow down to colleagues with whom the press dealt more kindly than himself, and he was only half pleased by their major productions. He abhorred Goncharov's *Precipice*; about *War and Peace* he said, "There are many beautiful things in it but also many horrors. It is heartrending when an autodidact of Tolstoy's stamp sets out to philosophize. He mounts some hobbyhorse, invents some oversimplified system that is supposed to solve everything so effortlessly—historical fatalism, for example—and forward march! But when he comes down to earth, like Antaeus, all his powers are restored to him."[16]

He himself felt little inclination to write. The public's lukewarm, not to say hostile, response to *Smoke* was no encouragement to begin a new novel. So he confined himself to publishing short stories—"An Unfortunate Woman," "King Lear of the Steppe"—and literary reminiscences.

The adulation of him and his work that he was so sorry to have lost in Russia was still alive in France, where the circle of his relations among men and women of letters had widened considerably. He was now quite close to Flaubert, Sainte-Beuve, George Sand, and others. The French saw him as an incarnation of Russia—while the Russians were rejecting him as a deserter. He saw Herzen several times in Paris, where the exile was seriously ill. His death was announced soon afterward. "Whatever the differences in our opinions, whatever our quarrels, the man who has died was an old comrade, an old friend," he wrote to Annenkov. "Our ranks are thinning. Everybody in Russia, no doubt, will say he ought to have died sooner, he has outlived himself. But what do such words signify, what does all our work signify, in regard to the silent abyss that will soon engulf us? As though living, continuing to live, were not the one essential question for a man."[17]

Also in Paris, he was invited by Maxime du Camp to observe the preparation for death and execution of a mechanic named Jean-Baptiste Troppmann who had murdered a family of eight. He was horror-stricken. "I shall not forget that dreadful night when I supp'd full of horrors and acquired a permanent aversion for capital punishment in general and the way it is carried out in France in particular,"[18] he wrote to Annenkov. At once, in a long article titled "Troppmann's Execution," he gave a detailed account of the preparations for the execution. His overriding impression was one of shared guilt, shared by the condemned man and the whole of society. He felt covered in shame, bathed in blood, by this legalized murder. "The feeling of some serious, unknown sin and secret shame grew within me apace," he wrote. "Perhaps I should link this feeling to the fact that the horses harnessed to the wagon, which were peacefully munching oats, seemed to be the only innocent creatures present."[19]

For once, the ways of the West revealed themselves to his eyes as more barbaric than those of Russia. Shaken to the core by what he had witnessed at the prison and on the place de la Roquette, where the guillotine was erected, he hurried back to Russia. He did not find the solace he hoped for there. He stayed just long enough to greet a few friends, read them his latest works, sell one hundred and twenty acres of land, and give a party at Spasskoye to divert the *muzhiks,* before leaving the country once more for Baden-Baden.

There he sank happily back into the cozy warmth of the Viardot family. He had his intellectual friendship with the husband, his platonic love for the wife, his paternal affection for the children, especially Claudie—his dear little Didie—whose freshness and spontaneity enchanted him. "I truly worship that creature, so charming, pure, graceful," he wrote to Pauline Viardot in 1868. "I positively melt when her image comes into my mind and I hope that Heaven has its finest blessings in store for her."[20]

All the Viardot children showed promise in the arts. Claudie was a gifted musician, as was Marianne, and also painted prettily. Paul, now thirteen, was being schooled for a brilliant career as an international violinist. Turgenev, convinced of his future as a virtuoso, made him a present of a Stradivarius. Louise, the eldest, who had become Madame Ernest Héritte in 1862, was an excellent pianist, had a fine voice, and would herself perform in public and teach singing. But she was a difficult woman and since childhood had hated Turgenev's constant presence around her mother.* The one he was closest to, beyond any doubt, was Claudie. Her power over him was ambiguous, as can be seen from his letters, while her response to his doting affection was a childlike and inoffensive coquetry. He was tickled, as so often in the past, by this mixture of physical attraction and moral prohibition. When Claudie married, he provided her with a comfortable dowry, and her appeal to him as a young married woman became even greater than before. "And now, Madame," he wrote to her, "imagine yourself sitting on the edge of the billiard table and myself standing in front of you; you are swinging your pretty feet, as you so often do; I catch them and kiss them, one and then the other, then your hands, then your face, and you let me because you know there is no one in the whole world whom I adore more than yourself."[21]

The bucolic peace of Baden-Baden was soon disrupted by anguish and consternation, however. Everyone was alarmed by the sudden declaration of war between France and Prussia. Turgenev learned of it when passing through Berlin on his way back from Russia. He began to wonder if, in returning to Germany, he wasn't throwing himself into the lion's den. The country would surely be laid to waste, torn and bloodied by battles. People were saying that the army of Napoleon III was invincible. Should he run to Russia, or England, to

*In 1907 Louise Héritte published some reminiscences that were both malicious and highly inaccurate as far as Turgenev's relations with her parents were concerned. Her son republished them, under the title *Une famille de grands musiciens. Mémoires de Louise Héritte-Viardot* (1922).

get out of danger? His daughter, Paulinette, was begging him to leave while there was still time. He replied, with some pride: "Rail communications have been cut. The bridge at Kehl has been blown up. There is a rumor that the French have crossed the Rhine. We shall probably have many wounded here. But that is no reason why I should abandon my friends and find some safe place for myself to hide in. I can understand that at the first moment you might have written as you did, but you will see, if you think about it, that a man of honor cannot act otherwise than I have decided to do. So, patience and more patience. Here I stay."[22]

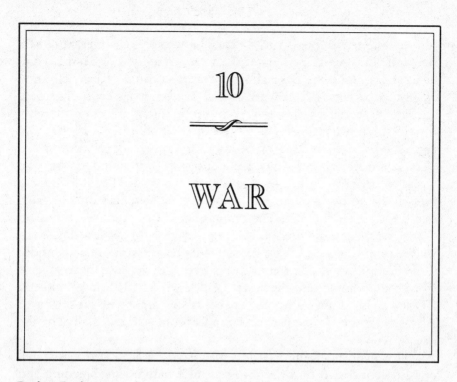

10

WAR

Baden-Baden was close to the frontier. The military reputation of the French was such that Turgenev expected to see them crossing the Rhine at the very start of the war. "Baden-Baden is absolutely empty," he wrote to his brother, Nicholas. "But I'm staying here, even if the French do come. What can they do to me?"[1] Five days later, having consulted the Viardots, he changed his mind, and told a friend, Mrs. Milyutin, "We're ready for anything; if need be, we shall leave for Wildbad by coach, since all rail communications have been cut. I say 'we,' meaning the Viardot family and myself. I shall not part from them."

Like the Viardots, Turgenev was fiercely opposed to the Napoleonic government and feared a French victory, which would mean an increase of despotism in Europe. Therefore, despite his sympathies for the land of Flaubert and George Sand, he was hoping that the German army would win, and the first French defeats accordingly drew sighs of relief from him. Even with all the windows shut tight, they could hear the cannonfire in the distance. The ladies of Baden-Baden were knitting vests for the wounded. Every good report from the front set the town's bells ringing wildly. Turgenev wrote to Borisov, "I rejoice at the defeat of France because it means the death knell of the Napoleonic empire, the existence of which is incompatible with the progress of freedom in Europe."[2] A little later he wrote to the German historian and philologist Friedländer, "I need not tell you again that I am, heart and soul, on the German side. This is a positive war, civilization against barbarians . . . Bonapartism must be shown the error of its ways . . . The 'great nation' has proved so hateful, mendacious, profoundly rotten!"[3] He halfheartedly deplored the bombing of Strasbourg and applauded the surrender of Sedan and capture of Napoleon III: "These are not events, they are a succession of thunderbolts," he wrote to his new friend, the German writer and illustrator Ludwig Pietsch. "Another roar deafens us before we have had time to catch our breath after the last. The emperor and one hundred thousand French prisoners, the republic! . . . Perhaps in another few days Paris will be captured and Ludwig Pietsch will proceed triumphantly under the Arc de l'Etoile . . . I consider it a real joy to have been able to witness the plunge into the sewer of that wretched scum [Napoleon III] and all his clique. Why are they being so lenient with the creature? All he deserves is to be packed off to Cayenne and eaten alive by the lice."[4]

However much the Viardots may have rejoiced at the downfall of Napoleon III, it hurt them to see their native land bleeding and humiliated. They thought the punishment should have been meted out to the emperor alone and that the nation as a whole should be spared. Turgenev, following their example, no longer knew whether to sing hymns to German omnipotence or commiserate with fallen France. The Germany he was accustomed to venerating was the Germany of poets and scholars, a sentimental, idyllic, peace-loving place. The Germany he was now beginning to perceive was bellicose, brutal, and domineering. He had no love for Napoleon III; but was he supposed to kneel down to William I and Bismarck? As the days passed, the Viardots felt more and more uncomfortable in their position as French residents in German Baden-Baden. At length, they packed their bags and went to London, where Turgenev soon joined them. In the first weeks of hostilities, he had sent the *St. Petersburg News* a "Correspondence" on the subject of the Franco-Prussian war, which had been distinctly Germanophile in tone. Now, undecided as ever, he found that he cared more for the defeated French than the victorious Germans. Since Russia had taken no part in the war, he could keep partisan passions out of the way. He was by no means neutral, but the outcome of the military operations was not, for him, a matter of life or death. He found himself in his favorite position, that of international onlooker.

He had hoped for some cheering news from Russia; but in his own words his latest story, "King Lear of the Steppe," had been a "fiasco." This time even the "ordinary reader" was not with him. "It is no great disaster," he told Annenkov. "But I am afraid this series of failures may have a negative effect on the publisher and make him reluctant to pay me four hundred rubles a page, and I can't take less . . . So henceforth I am going to write solely 'for friends,' to use the expression adopted by retired men of letters; or, more surely, I shall not write at all . . . The war has ruined the Viardots and Madame Viardot must try to earn money in England, the only place in which that commodity still exists."[5]

His experience of London was cold, fog, and an empty purse; and of late he had also been having painful attacks of gout. Pauline Viardot gave singing lessons, at one hundred francs an hour. And, although she had retired from the stage, she now valiantly decided to resume her career. Indefatigably, she scheduled more or less poorly paid recitals here, there, and everywhere. The doting Turgenev wondered at her vitality, her gaiety, her organizational ability. He, meanwhile, found life in England both busy and bleak, and made no effort to associate with the writers of the day. Seen from London, events in France were heartbreaking. The capture of Orléans and Rouen, the French retreat beyond the Marne, were so many blows at the Viardot family and himself. "I was deeply grieved but not surprised by the news from France," he wrote to Pauline Viardot, who was away on a concert tour. "I have stopped believing in the outcome of this conflict and see it as nothing more than the gradual extermination of France, the Republic, and freedom." And then came a sigh: "In addition to the profound and inalterable feeling that I have for you, it has now become somehow impossible for me to exist without you: your absence makes me physically anxious, as though I lacked air to breathe, it is a throbbing, hidden worry I cannot get rid of, and nothing can take my mind off it. When you are there I am quietly happy, and I feel right, and at home, and want nothing more."[6] Another source of concern was his daughter, Paulinette. Her husband, Gaston Bruère, had been ruined by the war. She was desperate. "I hope you will emerge from this ordeal better and stronger than before," he wrote her, "and in any case you must know that you have a father who will never allow you to want for bread."[7] But he was short of money himself. The only solution was to sell more land. But to do that, he had to go to Russia. And Russia was appealing to him less and less.

He made up his mind at last and disembarked, reluctantly, in St. Petersburg. He was there when he first heard of the peace terms imposed upon France: "And so Alsace and Lorraine are lost; five billions!" he wrote to Pauline Viardot. "Poor France! What a hideous blow; how can it be repaired? I immediately thought of you and what you must be feeling . . . Peace at last, but what a peace! Everyone here is full of sympathy for France, but that only makes it all the more bitter."[8]

Still feeling sincerely sorry for France, for Paulinette, and for his friends the Viardots, he nevertheless went dutifully about his customary round of social obligations, attended dinner parties, theaters and concerts, and sat for painters. Before leaving for England, he commissioned a friend, Maslov, to sell a piece of property for him, at any price. He had hardly reached London before he learned of the latest blow dealt him by Dostoyevsky, in the form of a caricature of himself in his new novel *The Possessed*. One of the characters in the book, the author Karmazinov, was presented as a "European Russian," and in his mouth Dostoyevsky put the very words of the author of *Smoke*: "I have become a German and I congratulate myself." To sharpen the resemblance between portrait and model, Dostoyevsky endowed his character with a "florid complexion, thick curls of white hair flowing about his top hat and twining around his small, clean pink ears." And he gave him a honeyed and slightly whinnying voice. His vanity wounded, Turgenev reacted with dignity. "I am told Dostoyevsky has caricatured me . . . Well, may he have a good laugh!" he wrote to Polonsky.

The events of the Paris Commune made his hair stand on end. An insurrectional government, riots, brother slaying brother under the sneering eye of the Germans! "I am in England, not for pleasure but because my friends [the Viardots], who have been virtually ruined by this war, have come here to earn a little money,"[9] he wrote to Flaubert; and asked him how he had weathered the "ghastly storm." Had he managed to remain a "born spectator"? When he learned that the Parisian revolutionaries had been crushed by Thiers's troops and of the dreadful reprisals that had followed, he had a thought that he noted in the margin of a manuscript: "This is still not the end and it is not a beginning. It was a mess and it will remain a mess. *Finis Franciae!*" But at the same time he was hoping that once peace was restored by the victory of the conservative forces, he would finally be able to return to France and see his daughter and friends again. "These events in Paris have absolutely staggered me," he wrote, again to Flaubert. "I have kept silent the way one is silent on a train when the train enters a tunnel: the infernal racket fills you and shakes your wits loose. Now that it has more or less subsided, I want to tell you that I shall very certainly come to see you."[10] And after making a speech in English, in Edinburgh, on the occasion of the jubilee for Walter Scott, and after keenly enjoying a partridge shoot in Scotland, he embarked for the continent on August 16.

Passing briefly through Paris, he could see that life in the bruised capital was returning to normal; then he was off to Baden-Baden where the Viardots were selling all they had, intending to leave Germany for good. Since he was quite incapable of imagining life without them, Turgenev also sold the house he had just finished building, in which he had hoped to end his days. According to the terms of the sale agreement, he was to quit the premises on November 1, 1871. He spent his last weeks in Germany in bed, nursing a violent attack of gout. To kill time, he worked at a long story, "Spring Torrents," in which there was not one word of politics.

In this story the stage is once again occupied by the overpowering force of love, the radiant mastery of the woman and cringing abasement of the man, enfeebled by the intensity of his emotions. The work is profoundly Turgenevian in the elegance of its style and the fatalism of its theme. Its author was, accordingly, moderately pleased with it. But as always, he feared its reception in the Russian press, which had such scant patience with him.

He was also worried about the atmosphere he would find in France. "What strikes me most in the present Assembly in France," he wrote to the French publisher Jules Hetzel, "is its lack of patriotism in the simplest and truest sense of the word. When the shame of foreign occupation should be their one thought day and night, should sear them unbearably like a hot iron attached to their boot soles and their hearts and souls, these gentlemen spend their energy debating questions of parties, governments, heaven knows what. In truth, it is demeaning France tremendously in the eyes of Europe . . . If Thiers has the right to be where he is, it is because, when all is said and done, one cannot help feeling in him that patriotism of which I have been speaking."[11]

The Viardots left first; Turgenev rejoined them in Paris on November 21, 1871. The family and the family's friend moved into the Viardots' town house at 48, rue de Douai. The gale had blown itself out; the Viardots heaved a sigh of relief as they recovered their furniture, their friends, and their bank account. Never had Turgenev felt closer to the loved one. She and her husband occupied the ground floor, with drawing room, dining room, and concert hall, the chief feature of which was a monumental organ, and a picture gallery containing many masterworks by such painters as Velázquez, Ribera, Guardi, and so on. Louis Viardot was a discerning collector. A carved wooden staircase led up to the top floor, where four rooms were set aside for the author. The walls of his study were hung with green cloth, everything in it was neatly in its place (he hated mess and disorder); there were two main pieces of furniture in the room—a table for writing and a divan for naps. Books everywhere—Russian, French, English, German. On the walls were a landscape by Theodore Rousseau, a Corot, a profile of Pauline Viardot in marble bas-relief, and a cast of the singer's hand with its tapering fingers. The better to hear her when she sang, he had an acoustical tube installed from his study to the music room. This contrivance cost him two hundred francs. He called it his "telephone," and Pauline said, "It's Turgenev's ear." That way, even when she was not physically present she remained a living part of the work and dreams of her tireless admirer.

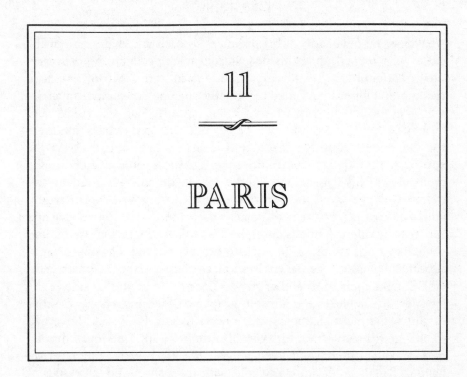

11

PARIS

The house at 48, rue de Douai quickly became a rallying point for Russians living in Paris. To them, Turgenev was an "ambassador of intelligence." Known and unknown callers turned up at all hours without bothering to announce themselves. Some came to see him out of curiosity, others to submit a manuscript, others to appeal for funds for some revolutionary publication. He received them all with the same weary courtesy, listened to their tales, promised his support, and, in private, railed against their lack of common manners. But although he kept saying that this incessant and importunate coming and going was not to be borne, inwardly he needed to see and hear them. Through them he felt that he remained in some sort of touch with Russia, caught a breath of its sustaining air. It was another way of continuing to be Russian in France. Sometimes, while conversing with his émigré fellow countrymen, the sounds of a piano would rise up and fill his study. Pauline Viardot was singing downstairs. He would listen intently, a rapt, childlike smile on his lips. Then, looking only half-awake, he would give a guilty start and return to the conversation. His passion for the robust fifty-four-year-old matron with the graying hair, huge dark eyes, and indomitable personality did not prevent him from taking a real interest in the little Russian colony in Paris. With a sense of duty made up of intermingled patriotism, generosity, and weakness, he never forgot his promises to each and every one of the exiles who turned up on his doorstep in search of a crumb of solace. He conscientiously read every shoddy manuscript, wrote letters of recommendation, intervened personally on behalf of some compatriot who was ill and having trouble being admitted to a hospital, lent money knowing it would never be repaid, arranged musical matinées for the needy, founded the first Russian library in Paris.* At the approach of old age, his mind reverted increasingly often to the memories of his Russian childhood; his daydreams were fed by this rich and diverse wellspring from the past. Closing his eyes, he would amble along the paths at Spasskoye or the streets of St. Petersburg and Moscow, inhale the smells and hear the voices of a far-off world; and yet he was not eager to go back. Here everything was appearance, superficial pleasure, genial civilization; the harsh reality in which great works strike their roots and grow was back there on the far side of the frontier. And so he found himself incapable of writing a novel or story in which the main characters were not Russian. He would have had to change his soul, if not his skin. "If I am to work," he told Edmond de Goncourt one day, "I need winter, the kind of freezing cold we have in Russia, a biting, tangy cold with trees shrouded in crystals of frost . . . And yet I work even better in the autumn, you know, on those days when there is no wind, not a single breath of air, and the ground is elastic and there is a sort of winey taste in the air . . ." De Goncourt added, "Turgenev did not complete his sentence, but a spasm passing through the fists clutched to his chest told us what an intensity of pleasure and mental intoxication he experienced in this little corner of old Russia."[1]

All of Turgenev's French friends had commented upon the powerful streams of mystery and melancholy that emanated from this "grand old man" of fifty-seven with the silky white beard, thick silvery hair, large, strong nose, and sentimental gaze. They ascribed his subtle charm to his Slavic origins.

Turgenev was a permanent fixture in the French literary world, and had long known and admired George Sand. More recently he had become friendly with Gustave Flaubert, and at the "Magny dinners" or in other restaurants he also met Sainte-Beuve, Edmond de Goncourt, Théophile Gautier, Taine, Renan, and others. During one dinner at the Véfour, Edmond de Goncourt bent his eagle eye upon

*The library, bearing Turgenev's name, was completely dismantled by the Germans during the 1940–44 occupation of Paris but has since been reconstituted.

his table companions. "Madame Sand was more mummified than ever, but full of kindliness and the gaiety of a woman of the last century," he wrote that evening. "As is his wont, Turgenev was talkative, expansive, and everyone else fell silent so that the soft-voiced giant could tell his stories, made moving by delicate little touches of emotion."[2] A few young writers—Daudet, Zola, Maupassant—had recently joined the older group. But of all these distinguished colleagues, the one Turgenev liked far the most was Flaubert. "There was a bond, an affinity of naïve goodheartedness, between those two large personalities," Alphonse Daudet wrote later in *Trente Ans de Paris*. "It was George Sand who married them. Flaubert, vainglorious and irreverent, a Don Quixote with a stentorian voice, a powerful irony in his every observation, something of the Norman of the Conquest in his bearing, was the virile half of this union of souls; but who could have guessed, in that other colossus with the eyebrows of tow and the huge features, the presence of a woman, that woman of nervous refinement whom Turgenev portrayed in his books, that edgy, exhausted, intense Russian woman, somnolent as a harem inmate, tragic as the elements in revolt? How true it is that in the muddle of the great human factory, souls often get attached to the wrong wrappings, the souls of men in ingenues' bodies, women's souls in cyclopean carcasses." Turgenev appreciated the frankness, openness, the bluff ways and honesty of the great rogue elephant of Croisset, with his hatred of stupidity, his contempt for society, his scorn of conventions and affectations. Flaubert had no fear of criticism, illness, or death. He had struggled free from the clutches of women. He was fed and devoured by his art. With him, Turgenev felt curiously soft, indefinite, irritable, vulnerable. Flaubert had "determined" his own life to be as it was, while Turgenev's life had been "determined" by somebody else. Flaubert was his own master, Turgenev never more than half his own man. Flaubert stood fast in the gale, Turgenev tended to bend with the breeze. When Flaubert wrote he chipped and chiseled away at his sentences and, to make certain they were perfect, put them through the "throat" test; Turgenev was more concerned to achieve simplicity, fluency, harmony. All the same, the two men shared a virtually religious worship of literature. Turgenev would call on Flaubert in his lair at Croisset or his little apartment decorated in the Algerian manner on the rue Murillo in Paris, overlooking the parc Monceau. On Sundays, noisy gatherings took place there, attended by Turgenev (nicknamed "le bon Moscove"),

Daudet, Zola, de Goncourt, Maupassant. Flaubert would play the host in a gandoura, with a fez on his head, and the occasions were characterized by a great freedom of manners, opinions, and language.

Flaubert's fraternal feeling for Turgenev is constantly being expressed in his correspondence. Letter after letter is filled with praise of "le Moscove": "This Scythian is a gigantic fellow," he wrote on May 25, 1873. "I like him better and better," he stated on December 30, 1873. And in January 1873, "Madame Sand is now the only literary friend I have, apart from Turgenev. But the two of them are as good as an army." On October 5, 1873, he wrote: "He's an exquisite man. You can't imagine what he knows . . . I do believe he knows *every* literature, down to its very toes! And so unpretentious withal! So easygoing, and such a sloth! Ever since I wrote him that he was a 'soft pear' he has not been known by any other name at the Viardots'."

So, while praising Turgenev's exceptional merits, Flaubert did not shrink from pointing out his weaknesses. The reproaches most frequently voiced related to his subservience to Pauline Viardot, and his shillyshallying every time he had a decision to make. "The Muscove is so thoroughly enslaved that I have no idea whether he is at Bougival, Saumur, or Oxford at the present moment," Flaubert wrote on September 9, 1873. And on December 20, 1876, "What a rarity is a straight line! What harm would it do him [Turgenev] to finish what he starts? But no, he dawdles, keeps putting things off."

When Turgenev was with these companions whom he admired and respected, he would talk endlessly about Russia. Thanks to him, they became acquainted with the works of Pushkin, Gogol, and Tolstoy. He also taught them about the Russian way of life, Russian landscapes, Russian history. To them he was an ideal interpreter between France and a vast, unknown place full of enigmas and promise. He was so sincerely devoted to his fellow Russian authors that he worked like a dog, without a grain of jealousy, to get their works translated into French. And when those works were successful in France he was as happy as if he had won some battle all by himself. At the same time, he recommended French works to Russian publishers for translation. Among others, he personally translated Flaubert's *Temptation of Saint Anthony, Herodias,* and *Legend of Saint Julian Hospitaller.* He found a justification for his continued presence on foreign soil in this role as propagandist in the service of two cultures at once. He rationalized his self-exile by telling himself that he was not living in France for his own pleasure only, but was making himself useful to both his native and his adopted lands. Russian literature was not the only one he touted to his friends, moreover; he was much more of a European than any of them, and spoke German, English, Italian, and Spanish as well as Russian and French. One Sunday afternoon at a gathering at Flaubert's, he translated Goethe's "Prometheus" and "Satyros" to his dazzled audience, reading straight from the book. "The parc Monceau sent up its children's voices, bright sunlight, fresh scent of newly watered lawns," wrote Alphonse Daudet, "while we four, Goncourt, Zola, Flaubert and myself, staggered by this grandiose improvisation, sat listening to genius being translated by genius."[3]

Not only did Flaubert respect his "bon Muscove" as an author; he also regarded him as his best literary adviser. "Yesterday I spent a good day with Turgenev, to whom I read the hundred and fifteen pages of *Saint Anthony* which have been completed thus far," he told George Sand. "After that, I read him about half of the *Dernières Chansons*. What an ear! And what a critic! He overwhelmed me by the depth and acuity of his judgment. Ah, if only all the people who dabble in judging books could have heard him, what a lesson for them! Nothing escapes him. At the end of a hundred-line passage he can remember one weak adjective. For *Saint Anthony* he gave me two or three exquisite bits of advice on specific details."[4]

Maupassant described Flaubert "listening to Turgenev as though in church, fixing upon him his blue eyes with the mobile lids and answering the soft, feeble voice with his own trumpet-blast, that breaks like a bugle-call from beneath the moustaches of the old Gaulic warrior." And on March 2, 1872, Edmond de Goncourt sketched this portrait of the "bon Muscove": "From the very first course at dinner Turgenev, the gentle giant, the lovable barbarian with his white hair falling into his eyes, the deep groove barring his forehead from side to side like a plow furrow, and his childlike talk, charmed us, *engarlanded* * us as the Russian expression is, with his mixture of candor and subtlety—all the allure of the Slavic race but heightened in him by the originality of a superior mind, by vast and world-embracing knowledge." That evening at Flaubert's Turgenev told his friends, "If I were vain about such matters, I should ask only that it be inscribed on my tomb what my book [*Memoirs of a Sportsman*] did for the emancipation of the serfs. Yes, that is all I should ask. Tsar Alexander made it known to me that my book was one of the great factors in his decision."[5]

*Wrapped round us like honeysuckle, perhaps—T.N.

Soon the little group decided to dine together regularly once a month. They called this the "Flaubert dinner" or the "booed writers' dinner" because every one of them claimed to have been booed in the theater at least once, for some play he had written. It wasn't true of Turgenev, but he insisted that it was in order not to disappoint his companions. Sometimes the dinner would be held at Adolphe and Pelé's place behind the Opéra, sometimes in a tavern near the Opéra-Comique that was famous for its bouillabaisse, and sometimes at Voisin's. They all called themselves gastronomes, but their tastes differed. Flaubert thrilled to the flavors of Rouen duckling cooked à l'estouffade, Edmond de Goncourt thought it the last word in elegance to chew on candied ginger, Zola doted on sea urchins and shellfish, while Turgenev spooned down his caviar. "Nothing could be more delicious than dinners among friends at which people can speak openly, their wits alert and their elbows on the table," wrote Alphonse Daudet. "We would sit down to the table at seven, and at two in the morning we were still at it. Flaubert and Zola dined in their shirtsleeves, Turgenev reclined on a divan, we sent the waiters away— a wholly useless precaution, since Flaubert's 'bugle' could be heard from attic to cellar—and we talked literature . . . There was always a book by one or the other of us that had just come out . . . We talked absolutely frankly, without flattery and without the complicity of mutual admiration."[6]

When they had finished their discussion of their own and other people's books, they moved on to more general topics. Often, in this group of men who had dined and drunk abundantly, the main subject was love. For Zola, Maupassant, Flaubert, and Edmond de Goncourt, love was first and foremost a physical phenomenon. They explored the subject with zest and appetite, the way they explored and consumed their fine food. Their bawdier remarks were punctuated with shouts of laughter. Turgenev, on the other hand, saw the union of a man and a woman as a manifestation of the supernatural. "I approach a woman," he told his friends, "with no other sentiment but respect, I am moved and amazed by my good fortune."[7] Edmond de Goncourt also noted, "He [Turgenev] said that love had an effect on men that was produced by no other emotion; it was as if, in someone who was truly in love, he were taken out of himself. He spoke of a weight in the heart in which there was nothing human. He spoke of the eyes of the first woman he loved as of some utterly immaterial thing, having no aspect in common with physical being . . . In all this there is just one problem, and it is that neither Flaubert, despite all his exaggerated speeches on these matters, nor Zola, nor myself, has ever been very seriously in love, and we are incapable of portraying love. Turgenev alone would be capable of that."[8] It was to Pauline Viardot that Turgenev dedicated his hymns to love, although he never named her. Surrounded by all these dyed-in-the-wool "realists" swollen with bestial appetites, he fancied himself a virtually disincarnate being, on the verge of rejecting the fleshly envelope altogether. Did this have something to do with his age? No; as far back as he could remember he had been the same, a romantic who had strayed into the wrong time and place. All his life he had been drawn to the mystery of woman. Every woman was for him a universe to be discovered, and so he went, from exploration to exploration, ecstasy to ecstasy. But he was not a strongly sensual person, so he was more eager to share the raptures of the soul with his partners than those of the body.

One evening Théophile Gautier heaved himself up from the table, fell back onto a divan, and moaned, "The truth of it is that I can no longer be interested by anything, it seems to me that I no longer belong to this day and age . . . I feel as though I were already dead!" "What I feel," said Turgenev, "is not quite that. You know how sometimes there is an imperceptible musty scent in an apartment that one cannot get rid of, drive away . . . Well, around me, all the time, there is something like a scent of death, the void, dissolution."[9] And yet he claimed he was not afraid of dying. "Oh, death, I never think about it," he told Daudet. "None of us Russians can imagine it very clearly, it is always far away and shrouded . . . the Slavic mists." And Daudet added, "The Slavic mists drift over everything he has ever written, blur it, and make it shimmer and tremble, and his very conversation is also somehow aqueous."[10]

In Turgenev's life, and in his writing, the "Slavic mists" were thickening from year to year. As he grew older, his perception of the superterrestrial realm became keener. On several occasions he had had hallucinations and did not know what to make of them. One time, coming downstairs on his way to dine, he saw Louis Viardot in shooting garb washing his face in his dressing room; then, as he entered the dining room a few steps beyond, he saw the same Louis Viardot sitting quietly in his usual place. Or again, in London once, he was conversing with a pastor and suddenly perceived the other man's skeleton standing beside him, with jutting jaw and gaping sockets. Another time, on a sunny morning, it was the ghost of an unknown woman wearing a peignoir who came to him and spoke to him in French. Although he professed to be an agnostic, he admitted that these visions were influencing his life and work. A peculiar duality showed in both his personality and creation: Alongside the everyday, clear-headed, reasoning fellow with both feet on the ground stood the man of the night, besieged by premonitions and blinded by mirages. Alongside the everyday novels, well built, solid and clear, stood the nocturnal stories shimmering in enigma. While rejecting the teachings of the established church, Turgenev was becoming increasingly con-vinced of the existence of another world. At times he felt enveloped in a breath from the beyond. Then he would seek release from his anguish by writing tales such as "Phantoms" or "The Dog" or "Knock, Knock, Knock" or "The Watch." The author himself thought the last of these stories was "strange" and the one after it, "The Dream," was an actual nightmare described with diabolical precision and boldness. Rape, the obsession of the guilty father, be-witchment, magic—Turgenev was giving free rein to fantasies that enchanted as they frightened him. In another story, "The Tale of Father Alexey," he analyzed the slow possession of a soul by the devil. Even that archetypally Russian masterpiece, "Living Relics," contains whiffs from beyond the grave. On March 5/17 Turgenev wrote in his diary, "Midnight. Sitting at my desk again. And in my soul it is night, blackest night . . . It's as though the grave were hastening to swallow me up. The empty day, objectless and colorless, passes like a flash. I have neither the right nor the desire to live. There's nothing more to do, nothing more to wait for, nothing more to want."

After these bouts of morbid melancholy he felt exorcised, purged. Life took hold again, he was happy to see his friends, buy paintings at the hôtel Druot, encourage the revolutionary enterprises of a man like Lavrov. What a curious character he was! Bakunin urged the intellectuals to go out to the people and incite them to immediate and total insurrection, whereas Lavrov, more modestly, was encourag-ing them to learn how the working classes actually lived so that they could educate and enlighten them, thereby preparing the way for the socialism of the future. In 1873 a wind of wild liberality, initiated by both these masters, was blowing over the youth of Russia. Young gentlemen and ladies felt an almost physical need to share the suffer-ings of the poor. An imperial decree was issued ordering Russian students in Switzerland to return to their homeland; consequently thousands of subversive-minded young propagandists came back from Europe and spread out into the countryside. People called them *narod-niks,* "populists." To play their new role, they donned coarsely woven, loose-fitting jackets, crumpled caps, and boots, and bade heroic farewells to their friends and families. Missionaries in the noblest of causes, they went to work as plowmen, laborers, boatmen. At the end of the day's work, they lectured the *muzhiks* on the need to dispossess the landowners and institute collective exploitation of the land. The mistrustful and mulish *muzhiks* took a dim view of these verbose lunatics with white hands who played at being their equals. Taught from birth to worship the tsar, scarred by centuries of slavery, the erstwhile serfs feared change in any form. Surely this was just another trap. Many times they themselves arrested the agitators and turned them over to the local authorities; the police were never more than one step behind the "populists."

Fascinated, Turgenev followed every turn and twist in this social phenomenon. He made several trips to Russia to observe it at first-hand. The product of his on-the-spot study was a novel dealing with the revolutionary intellectuals' "movement to the people," *Virgin Soil.* Nezhdanov and Marianne, the protagonists, are a young couple full of modern ideas who go out into the countryside to "evangelize" the masses and are given a home by Solomin, a factory manager who shares their political views. But Solomin, unlike the dreamers Nezhdanov and Marianne, is a practical man, levelheaded and self-assured. He knows how hard it will be to shake the dense wits of the *muzhik* herds into a new faith. He believes that the revolution is a necessity, but only in the distant future, after a gradual, moderate evolution of customs. Speaking to the common people, Nezhdanov soon comes to realize that he is talking a language of which they do not understand a single word. There is a continent separating him from these contemporaries whom he would like to indoctrinate and take into his arms. "I feel like a ham actor playing a part beyond his abilities," he says. In the end, the peasants, fed up with the speeches of these wooly agitators, turn them over to the authorities. Nezhdanov commits suicide while Marianne, who thought she loved him, betrays his memory and marries Solomin. Once again, as in *On the Eve,* the fervent young woman gives herself to the strong man. In portraying this new downfall of the daydreamer, the Russian Hamlet, Turgenev was condemning himself in the person of his hero.

The moment it was published, the book turned both revolutionaries and conservatives against him. The former were offended by his clearheaded, unindulgent analysis of the failure of one of their members, while the latter criticized the author for showing too much sympathy for a character like Solomin, whose opinions were distinctly subversive; middle-of-the-road critics said that the theme was presented too systematically and that Solomin lacked credibility, that like "the Bulgarian" before him, this character was the personification of an idea, a stiff-jointed wooden puppet. In the *Russian Review,* Peskovsky called *Virgin Soil* a hodgepodge of wrong ideas and artificial characters and said the hero's behavior was that of "children playing at revolution." Markov, writing in the *St. Petersburg News,* considered that the author had "disappointed the public's expectations of an artist" because the novel contained "neither poetic color nor true depth of character, nor even an attractive, lively plot." In *The Voice,* Markevich accused Turgenev of cruelty to "his Orthodox motherland." The critic of the *Bee* stung him with the comment that he could not have made any real study of his country's youth, so conventional was his presentation of its mentality and language. Turgenev was expecting this concert of protest. He wrote to Saltykov-Shchedrin, an impassioned liberal author, before the book was published: "I am not hoping for any laurel wreaths, only that my face won't be rubbed too hard in the mud."[11] And to Polonsky, "Whatever the fate of this book, it will be my last original work of literature. My decision is final. My name shall not appear again. So as not to lose the habit of using a pen, I shall occupy myself with translations."[12] Even so, he was hurt by the fury of some of his assailants. Disparaged in his own country, he suffered from the falseness of his position in France, the falseness of his position in relation to Russian youth, the falseness of his position in the family of Pauline Viardot. Wherever he turned he was a guest, a transient. The Russian soil he so loved had slipped out from under his feet. He was floating between two or three homelands, two or three languages, and belonged to none. He was a citizen of nowhere. His only consolation was the lavish and heartfelt praise of his French friends.

Patches of sunlight came, during this long Parisian eclipse, from his frequent meetings with the little group of French writers; from his trips to Croisset to see Flaubert, or to Nohant to see George Sand; from the birth of first a daughter and then a son to his daughter, Pauline Bruère—Jeanne and Georges-Albert; from Claudie Viardot's marriage to Georges Chamerot; and from the friendship of Lavrov, the exiled revolutionary whose paper, *En Avant* [*Forward*], he helped to subsidize. His own political views were becoming increasingly liberal. He accused France of being a pseudorepublic that had betrayed its own principles. After attending the session of the National Assembly at Versailles at which it was decided to extend the powers of the maréchal de Mac-Mahon, he wrote, to Flaubert, on November

19, 1873, "Well, my dear friend, since last night you have a military dictatorship. As people say, you are a Macmahonian. It has always seemed to me that being just plain French would be better, but I could be wrong . . . The day before yesterday I went to Versailles and came back revolted and heartsick."[13]

His fears of governmental abuse of power were shared by the Viardots, whose attitudes were in all circumstances openhanded and openhearted, independent and anticlerical. Their home soon became a focal point for cosmopolitans. They entertained all the big names in literary and artistic circles. Pauline Viardot, dressed almost always in elegant black lace, would sit down to her piano to sight-read a score someone had brought. Standing beside her with his pince-nez on his nose, Turgenev would read too. He had scant affection for the new trends in music and, according to Anton Rubenstein, who was a frequent guest, criticized some pieces angrily, in a high, "almost feminine" voice. Sometimes Claudie and Marianne would join their mother, delighting their hearers with three-part songs. On Sunday evenings there would be plays, dancing, improvised charades, and *tableaux vivants.* Turgenev adored these party games, but although they diverted him for a time they could not soften the bedrock bitterness in him. Apart from his concern over French politics and the frequent attacks of gout that prevented him from making any serious plans, there was always the nagging sense of being disliked in his own country. He went to Russia several times and each time came back disenchanted. In St. Petersburg, Moscow, even at Spasskoye, he no longer felt at home. It gave him a physical pleasure to sniff the air of his homeland and an intellectual nausea to endure the wordless reproaches of his compatriots. In 1872 he had had the weakness to allow the Maly Theatre in Moscow to put on his play *A Month in the Country,* which he had written twenty-two years before. It was panned by audience and press alike. Everyone agreed that it was a verbose and tedious work. "My play was to prove a fiasco," he told his brother, Nicholas. "That is why I have not written for the stage since 1851. It is not my place."[14] He himself was judged harshly in Russia, but he was quite capable of harshness in his own judgments of his Russian colleagues. He mistrusted best-sellers. Even Tolstoy's *Anna Karenina* he found disappointing. "With his talent, to stray into this high-society morass and flounder about in it, fussing and fretting and going nowhere, and to treat this twaddle not with humor but with high solemnity, to take it all seriously—what nonsense!" he wrote to his friend Toporov. "Moscow has destroyed him. He won't be the first or the last to whom that has happened, but I feel more sorry for him than for the others."[15]

On the strength of his long experience of women, he regarded himself as a sort of expert in affairs of the heart, which gave even greater weight to his scornful assessment of the woes of Anna Karenina, or so he felt. Even now—aging, weary, morose, and gout-ridden—he was dreaming of an emotional renaissance. Not content with worshipping Pauline Viardot, in late 1873 he became infatuated with the young aristocrat Julia Vrevsky. She was thirty-three, beautiful, free and impetuous, and her ideal was to live intensely in the company of some exceptional being. For a moment she thought she had found him in the famous fifty-six-year-old who read poetry aloud to her at Spasskoye and heaved long sighs as he kissed her hands. "There is no need for me to describe to you the somewhat strange but sincere and truthful feeling I had for you," he told her. "You know all that better than I do."[16] And also, "I always think that if we had met in our youth, when we were innocent and, most of all, free . . . complete the sentence yourself."[17] He saw her again in Paris, Karlsbad, and on another trip to Russia. On each occasion he regretted a little more deeply the humiliating constraints of his years. He longed for intimate, physical communion but his body would not respond. This conflict of soul and flesh was exhausting. To take his mind off it, he related to her the vicissitudes of his life as an unpopular author: "I regard my literary career as over. But one can live without literature and there are some things in life (especially with the advent of old age) that smart more painfully than any literary setback."[18] Another time he felt braver, and wrote, "I should like to spend a few hours with you, in your room, drinking tea and looking at the designs made by the frost on the windowpanes . . . No; ridiculous! . . . Looking at your eyes, I mean, which are so beautiful, and, now and then, kissing your hands, which are so beautiful—large, but that is the kind of hands I like."[19] And also, "I feel I am growing old . . . and it is not much fun. On the contrary. I want terribly, before all is over, to do something quite mad. Will you help me?"[20] Finally, still more explicitly, "Ever since I met you I have loved you as a friend; at the same time, I had an overpowering desire to possess you but I was no longer young and the desire was not fierce enough to impel me to propose marriage to you. Other considerations would have prevented that, moreover. But I also know that you would never consent to what the French call *une passade.* That is the explanation of my behavior. You want me to believe that you had no ulterior motives. Alas, I was only too well assured of the fact. You write that your woman's life is over; when my man's life is over—and I shall not have too long to wait—I am certain that we shall be great friends because there will be nothing more to disturb us. At this moment one thought arouses in me a feeling of burning anguish: what would have happened if she had held me to her breast other than fraternally? . . . There you have my confession."[21] The young woman was moved by the confession, but she too thought that their romance had come a little late. As always with Turgenev, love raveled away and sank into the sands. He mournfully tried to flog the dead horse: "There is no doubt that if, some while ago, you had wished . . . Now, alas, the time is past and this half-way period must be gone through as quickly as possible so that I can sail peacefully to the port of old age."[22]

Julia Vrevsky, however, was not the woman to sail her own ship peacefully "to the port of old age." Disappointed in love, she fell back upon action, with a vengeance. The instant war broke out between Russia and Turkey, she enlisted as a nurse and left for the front; she died of typhus, in Bulgaria. Turgenev was shaken by her death and dedicated a prose poem to her in which he described her death-agony on a bed of rotting straw in a shed surrounded by the soldiers she had been heroically nursing. Then, after this abortive attempt to escape from Pauline Viardot's enchanted circle, he went back, melancholy and bitter, and resumed his status as chief slave in the soprano's household.

12

TURGENEV AND TOLSTOY

"The Viardots and I have bought a wonderful villa here [at Bougival], a forty-five-minute drive from Paris," Turgenev wrote his friend Kolbasin on July 15/27, 1875. "I am having a pavilion built that will not be done until August 20, and I shall then move into it at once . . . My main residence is rue de Douai in Paris, and I go to town three times a week."

The villa was called "The Ashes" and stood on the banks of the Seine, from which one entered the grounds on paths covered in fine sand. Shrubs grew on all sides, along with weeping willows and ash trees with massive trunks; and there were statues, a fountain, murmuring brooks, a profusion of begonias, fuchsias, and roses on the lawns. The main house was tall, with an elegant white Directoire façade; that was for the Viardots. To the right, on a little knoll reached by a steep path, stood Turgenev's newly built chalet, in the Swiss manner, with pierced-wood balustrades on the balconies and greenery and flowers crowding close around it. On the ground floor were the dining room and drawing room. Above, a spacious study cluttered with books, paintings, and bric-a-brac. The chairs were upholstered in dark-red leather. Claudie's easel stood in one corner. She often came to paint some study or other in her "godfather's" room, while he looked on dotingly as she worked. From a corner window one could see the

Seine, its barges, fishing boats, and dingy taverns huddled beneath the willows and poplars. A few cows grazed in the nearby meadows, and beyond them the landscape dimmed into a bluish haze. Turgenev's bedroom was on the same floor, with his big canopy bed, his sofa, and his two tufted armchairs. Heavy drapes framed the windows. A balcony looked out onto the grounds. Above were rooms for guests and servants. With the first sunny days, the Viardots and Turgenev set out from Paris in a cortège of coaches laden with trunks, baskets, and boxes. The whole family came: Louis Viardot, now seventy-five, nodding on his seat; Pauline; her daughters Claudie Chamerot and Marianne; her son, Paul; a few of her pupils; the servants; the faithful Turgenev.

Life at Bougival was peacefully monotonous. Turgenev worked a bit, read a lot, went for little walks along the drives leaning on his stick, sat on a bench with a shawl around his shoulders and watched "the young people" playing croquet. In the evening he listened to Pauline Viardot and her pupils singing or played whist or chess until his head sank upon his chest. Before going to bed, he took a final turn around the garden, inhaled the smells of the slumbering countryside, gazed at the halo glowing over Paris in the distance, jotted a note or two in his diary. After one such walk he wrote, "The most interesting part of life is death."

He was often troubled by gout. When he was ill the whole family gathered around him. Claudie would paint, standing at her easel. Pauline did needlepoint, Marianne read some French or English novel aloud. Now and then Turgenev would put in a little joke, whereupon Claudie would put her small perfumed hand over his mouth and say, "Now, now, Tourgel [his nickname in the family], you just leave us in peace; we want to listen!" But despite all these signs of affection, his melancholy deepened day by day. The death of George Sand, in June 1876, affected him strongly. "Poor dear Madame Sand," he wrote to Flaubert. "She was fond of us both, especially you, and that was natural. What a heart of gold she had! What an absence of all petty, mean, trivial, false feelings, what a fine fellow she was, and what a tremendous woman! Now it is all in the ghastly, insatiable, mute, stupid hole that doesn't even know what it is devouring."[1] He wrote an obituary that was published in the *European Messenger.*

Sometimes Russian friends would come to call on him in his hideaway and talk about student unrest back home. As a partisan of freedom but an enemy to violence, he was upset and angered by all this disorderly agitation, which, in his opinion, could never lead to a democratic solution. Hundreds of young people were arrested at the "March to the People" and sent before judges. By giving them the right to defend themselves, this mass trial enabled the accused to attack the authorities and publicly enumerate all the advantages of revolution. Large excerpts from their inflammatory declarations were printed in the papers and reproduced *in toto* in booklets printed by clandestine presses. The authorities had imagined they were going to pillory the youthful "populists," when in fact they were giving them a platform, and public sympathy went out to these martyrs for the proletarian ideal. After that, students were forbidden to engage in peaceful propagandizing, so they took the next step, into action. Secret organizations sprang up all over the country. Workers in many factories went on strike. On December 6, 1876, in St. Petersburg, hundreds of workers and peasants demonstrated outside Our Lady of Kazan Cathedral. The police broke up the assembly brutally and arrested the leaders. Turgenev found the demonstration pointless and absurd. "Everything can be said to have a limit, except the imbecility of certain Russians,"[2] he wrote to his friend Stasulevich, the editor of the *European Messenger.* A few months later a twenty-nine-year-old woman named Vera Zasulich called on the chief of police, Trepov, and fired two shots at him, wounding him seriously. Arrested on the spot, she explained that she had wanted to kill Trepov because he had ordered one of the students picked up at the demonstration outside Our Lady of Kazan to be flogged. For what crime? For refusing to salute Trepov during a prison inspection. Her trial opened in an atmosphere of great tension. During the hearing, her lawyer stigmatized the brutality of the chief of police and extolled his client's high-mindedness. She was acquitted. The crowd pressing around the courthouse burst into applause and carried Vera Zasulich to Trepov's house in triumph. The Cossacks had to be called in to disperse the procession. Turgenev was appalled. He saw in these events the incoherent sequel to his novel *Virgin Soil.* "The Zasulich case has certainly set all Europe by the ears," he wrote to Stasulevich. "Yesterday, there was an article in *Le Bien public* headlined 'Let us celebrate our heroes.' And who are these heroes? Voltaire and Zasulich. From Germany I have received a pressing request to write an article on the trial, because all the newspapers see a close link between Zasulich and Marianne in *Virgin Soil.* I have even been nicknamed *der Prophet.* I naturally refused."[3] He was also very concerned by the Russian losses in the war with Turkey. "As far as I can see this is the result of our deplorable obsession with overrunning the Balkans instead of building up unattackable ramparts,"[4] he wrote to the same correspondent. It also pained him to see the countries he was fond of—France, Germany, and England—supporting the Ottoman cause. "The hardest thing of all," he told Annenkov, "is to see how the soul of every European, without exception, revels in our misfortunes. Even the French, the very French are rejoicing, when they ought to be wishing us all possible success."[5] And to Stasulevich again, "We Russians are feeling the same strain here as you back home. If peace comes soon, so much the better. If the war goes on, it will be dreadful. Not only the English and Germans, but even the French are quite rabid on the subject. On every side all one hears is, 'Barbarians! A barbarian invasion!' "[6] For the first time, he was feeling his isolation, his foreignness in a nation whose goodwill was essential to him. What was to become of him, unable as he was to spend more than a couple of months in succession in his native land, if France started hating the Russians? With a foot in each camp and a frontier down the middle, he feared for his international future and felt incapable of either lingering in a hostile atmosphere or leaving the country in which he had chosen to end his days.

Money from Russia came irregularly. The manager he had installed at Spasskoye was clearly robbing him. To supplement the income from his writing and the estate, Turgenev decided to sell some of his paintings at the Druot auction rooms. He was a well-known figure there, and had bought many a picture and bibelot in the days of his grandeur. The habitués of the place had nicknamed him "Monsieur Gogo" because he was such a novice about art. The results of his sale were not encouraging. "Although I am by no means ruined," he wrote to Polonsky, "my resources have so dwindled that I have been forced to sell my collection [of paintings]. I did so, and it was a disaster on the order of Sedan. I was expecting to lose six thousand francs overall but lost twelve thousand instead . . . The devil take all pictures. But I didn't sell my [Theodore] Rousseau."[7]

In the middle of all these annoyances came one great joy: the first letter from Tolstoy since their break.[8] "Ivan Sergeyevich," he wrote, "these past few days I have been thinking back over our relationship and I was surprised and happy to find that I had lost all my animosity toward you. Please God you feel the same. In fact, knowing how kindhearted you are, I am almost certain that your hostility died long before mine. If this is true, shall we shake hands, and will you consent to forgive me entirely and completely all the wrong I have done you? It is natural for me to remember only your best features, for you have been very good to me. I do not forget that it is to you that I owe my literary success and I also remember that you used to like what I wrote, and myself too. Honestly and openly, if you can forgive me, I offer you all the friendship of which I am capable. At our age, there is only one thing of value: the love we can share with our fellow men. I should be very happy if you and I could have such a relationship."[9]

This message of manly affection brought tears to Turgenev's eyes. After seventeen years of sulks, Leo Tolstoy was holding out his arms again. This kind of about-face was very much in the character of the master of Yasnaya Polyana, so quick to anger, to repent, to humiliate. It was his Russian blood that spoke in him when he flung himself into a confession in this way; none of Turgenev's French friends would have been capable, he thought, of so warmhearted a piece of folly. He replied: "Dear Leo Nikolayevich, the letter you sent to the post office to be left until called for did not reach me until today. It touched me deeply and made me very happy. It is my fondest wish to renew our former friendship and I most warmly shake your outstretched hand. You are quite right to think I have no hostile feelings about you. If I ever did, they vanished long ago; all that is left is a memory of a man to whom I was sincerely devoted, an author whose first works I had the good fortune to applaud before anyone else, and who continues to arouse my keenest interest with every new publication. I rejoice with all my heart and soul to see the end of the misunderstanding between us. I hope to go to Orel this summer and if I do we will surely meet again. In the meantime, I wish you all good things and, once again, cordially shake your hand."[10]

A few days later Turgenev's self-respect received another boost. He was chosen to act as vice-president of the International Literature Congress meeting in Paris. Victor Hugo was president. On June 4, 1878, Turgenev made a speech, in French, to his assembled colleagues, in which he hailed the contribution made by French literature to Russian culture: "Two centuries ago we were already moving toward you, without any clear understanding of you; one hundred years ago we were your disciples; today you have accepted us as your colleagues." The audience were charmed by his long silver locks, his impeccable attire, his pince-nez and the soupçon of a Russian accent in his voice, and applauded loud and long. Many of his works had already been translated in France, England, and Germany, and the press treated him with respect. Logically, his fellow countrymen should have interpreted his speech at the congress as Europe's homage to Russia. By making him vice-president, after all, the assembly had placed him on a level with Victor Hugo. The two authors had stood side by side, two patriarchs of the literary world, personifying the intellectual *entente* across their frontiers. But instead of that, the Russian papers rose up in arms against its representative at the congress who, according to them, should have extolled the Russianness of Russian literature, rather than humbly acknowledging its debt to the French. They said he had sycophantically demeaned his own country to aliens, they reproached him for failing to mention Tolstoy or Ostrovsky or Nekrasov or Saltykov-Shchedrin as great Russian authors of the century. Once again Turgenev felt misunderstood by his fellows. Whatever he did, whatever he said, there was a pack of detractors baying at his heels. He wrote to Toporov in despair, "If I could have foreseen the mudbath through which my compatriots would be dragging me because of the highly inoffensive speech I made, I should certainly not have taken part in the event, from which, moreover, nothing further has come."[11]

Despite this fresh falling out with his national press, he set out for Russia on July 21, 1878. After a brief pause in St. Petersburg and Moscow, he reached Tolstoy at Yasnaya Polyana on August 8. Tolstoy and his brother-in-law Stepan Behrs came to meet him at the Tula railway station. The two writers exchanged brotherly bear hugs and drove off together. At Yasnaya Polyana, Tolstoy's wife, Sonya, was delighted by the refined elderly giant with the snowy crest, the gentle, mournful gaze, and unctuous manners. The children gaped in wonder at the traveler's suitcases, his velvet waistcoat, silk shirt, paisley cravat, and soft leather pumps, his two gold chronometers and his snuff box. At dinner, he prattled fluently of the hectic and trivial life of Paris, his relations with French authors, his chalet at Bougival. His high voice contrasted oddly with his massive stature. In comparison, Tolstoy seemed short and squat, like a dumpy country hick and yet, at fifty, so surprisingly young. He was plainly making an effort to be polite to this person from Paris who pretended to be Russian. At one point, noticing that there were thirteen people at the table, Turgenev exclaimed, "Whoever is afraid of death, raise his hand!" And raised his own, with a laugh. Nobody dared follow suit, for fear of offending the Christian sentiments of the master of the house. "I seem to be the only one," Turgenev went on. Then, out of courtesy, Tolstoy stuck up his hand and grumbled, "Well, I don't like the thought of dying either!" Then, to change the subject, he asked his guest, "Why don't you smoke? You used to." "So I did," Turgenev answered. "But two charming young ladies in Paris told me they would not let me kiss them if I smelled of tobacco, so I stopped." Tolstoy's disapproval was ill dissembled, and his only response a chill silence.

After dinner the two men withdrew to the study for more serious talk. By tacit agreement they made no allusion to the quarrel that had divided them, but even on questions of literature and philosophy they were soon at loggerheads. Turgenev was not a believer and for him art was an end in itself. The service of beauty and truth was enough to justify a human life. For Tolstoy, a work of art had value only insofar as it contributed to its reader's moral uplift. He tried to make his elegant guest understand this, and lost patience when he could not convince him. Turgenev, who had lately begun to write a series of short, delightful prose poems, was increasingly sure that the dominant virtues of a modern author should be purity of style and accuracy of description—beliefs he shared with Flaubert. The more the crude and impetuous Tolstoy preached the need for a social message, the more the urbane and smiling Turgenev applauded the literature of delicacy, moderation, intelligence.

It was a fine day, so they went out into the garden where the rest of the family were awaiting them, curious but respectful. There was a seesaw near the house, formed by a plank laid across a chopping block. To amuse the children, the two men climbed onto the ends and began to move up and down; as one rose the other sank. Turgenev must have wondered whether there were not some hidden symbolism in this weighing of one, then the other, as if for posterity. After this diversion, they strolled through the surrounding meadows and woods. Turgenev, a nature lover, could identify every bird by its song: "There's a bunting!" he said. "And that's a linnet. A starling." But he was awed by Tolstoy's rapport with animals. Stopping near an old horse that was grazing by itself, he stroked its neck and murmured to it, translating, for Turgenev's benefit, what he thought the animal must have been feeling. "I could have listened to him forever," Turgenev later said. "He had got inside the very soul of the poor beast, and taken me with him. I could not refrain from remarking, 'I say, Leo Nikolayevich, you must have been a horse once yourself.' "[12]

That evening the family gathered in the drawing room while Turgenev read them his tale "The Dog." When he finished, their praises rang hollowly. Tolstoy did not really believe in the author's talent. Turgenev bent over backward to make himself agreeable, but Tolstoy could not forgive his Western airs, his indifference to religious issues, the superficiality of his conversation.

Turgenev was not aware of his host's impatience, and wrote to him, when he got back to Spasskoye, "I must tell you again how good and enjoyable it was for me to be at Yasnaya Polyana and how happy I am to see that the misunderstanding between us has vanished without a trace, as though it had never been. I felt very strongly that the years which have aged us were not lived in vain and that both of us have become better than we were sixteen years ago.* I hardly need tell you that I shall certainly stop by to see you again on my way back . . . This time, my feelings about Spasskoye are indefinite, neither sad nor joyful. It is as though I were somehow perplexed. Another sign of old age."[13]

On September 2, 1878, Turgenev returned to Yasnaya Polyana for three days and, with his customary candor, assumed that his host was delighted to see him again. He wrote to Fet, "It was a great joy for me to renew relations with Tolstoy . . . His whole family are most likable and his wife charming. He himself has calmed down considerably and matured. His name is beginning to spread throughout Europe. We Russians have long known that he has no rival."[14]

Tolstoy was not so enthusiastic. The day after Turgenev's departure, he too wrote to Fet: "Turgenev is the same as ever, and we have no illusions as to the degree of intimacy that is possible between us."[15] To the critic and philosopher Strakhov: "Turgenev has come back among us, amiable and brilliant as ever. But, between you and me, he is a little like a fountain filled with water that has been piped in from somewhere. One is always afraid that it is going to run dry and there will be nothing left."[16]

Upon rereading *War and Peace* Turgenev, who had previously had no good word to say for the book, now saw that it was worthy of survival. So, with renewed admiration and generosity, he set out, as soon as he returned to France, to promote his compatriot's international renown. First, he told Tolstoy how successful the English translation of *The Cossacks* had been, and what a pity it was that the same work had come out in a French adaptation by Baroness Mengden in *Le Journal de Saint-Pétersbourg.* He was a little put out by this because he was himself intending to translate *The Cossacks,* with the help of Pauline Viardot. "I don't know whether you have already made arrangements to publish it in book form in Paris," he wrote to Tolstoy, "but I should be very happy to assist the French public to appreciate the best story ever written in our language."[17]

This letter came at a bad time, when Tolstoy was going through

*Seventeen, actually.

one of his bouts of mystical humility and proclaiming that nothing he had ever written was fit to feed the pigs. He snapped back at his censer-bearer, "In spite of all my affection for you and my belief that you wish me well, I feel as though you, too, are mocking me. Therefore let us please not talk any more about my writing. You know that every man has his own way of blowing his nose, and believe me, I blow mine exactly as I see fit."[18] Disconcerted by this snort of peevish modesty seasoned with conceit, Turgenev replied, "Though you ask me not to speak of your writing, I cannot help pointing out that I have never, in the slightest degree, mocked you. I have liked some of your books enormously, disliked others intensely, and derived keen pleasure and genuine astonishment from still others, such as *The Cossacks.* But why should I have laughed at them? I thought you had long since freed yourself of such 'centripetal' feelings."[19]

This courteous but self-contained response infuriated Tolstoy, who told Fet, "Received an epistle from Turgenev yesterday. You know, I have decided to keep away from him and temptation. He really is an unpleasant trouble-seeker."[20] Identifying Turgenev with "temptation" seemed to justify Tolstoy's condemnation of the man, the very sight of whom set his teeth on edge. Turgenev, meanwhile, was continuing to exert himself on behalf of the French reputation of the man he thought of as his friend. In 1879, when the French translation of *War and Peace* came out, he launched a campaign, sent copies to all the major critics (Taine, Edmond About, and so on), rang every doorbell, orchestrated the triumph. "One can only hope they will grasp the full power and beauty of your epic," he wrote to Tolstoy. "I have recently been reading your very great work for the fifth or sixth time. Its structure is very foreign to everything the French are fond of and look for in a book, but the truth will prevail. I trust there will be, if not a smashing triumph, then a slow but sure conquest."[21] He sent Tolstoy a copy of the highly complimentary letter Flaubert had written about *War and Peace.* "It is first-rate. What a painter, what a psychologist!"

Once again the flowers fell upon stony ground. Tolstoy was sick and tired of praise. He had abandoned the futility of novel-writing and was dedicating himself to religion. But with his penchant for dissidence, isolation, and domination, he was thinking less of obeying the church than of defying its dogmas and ritual. Turgenev soon realized that Tolstoy was growing away from him again. It grieved him, but he continued to admire the great and intractable man.

Another character whose psychology Turgenev was unable to

fathom was the revolutionary Lavrov, who was a mixture of subversive audacity and naïve goodheartedness. "He's a dove that wants to be taken for a falcon," he wrote to Annenkov. "You should hear him proclaiming the need for another Pugachev uprising, a rebellion like that of Stenka Razin . . .* His words are pure thunder but his eyes are meek as a lamb, his smile affectionate; even his huge, bristling beard has something caressing and idyllic about it."[22]

In Russia, meanwhile, there was angry opposition to the government over the Berlin Treaty of July 1878, which marked the end of the Russian-Turkish war. The general opinion was that the treaty was a slap in the fatherland's face. Why had the Slavic provinces of Bosnia and Herzegovina been ceded to Austria? Why had Bulgaria been partitioned? Why hadn't the army been allowed to enter Constantinople? The military accused the diplomats of stealing their victories. The press fulminated against Germany and England for betraying Russia. The young intellectuals were becoming increasingly defiant of the government, whose international setbacks made its domestic blunders seem worse. Turgenev was frightened by these young intellectuals, yet he was irresistibly drawn by their fervor. He would have given much to win their confidence; but they simply were not interested in him. Plainly, his day was done.

When he looked back over his career, though, he could not help feeling a little pride. In his novels he had portrayed nature better than anyone else, he had created a few unforgettable, fully rounded characters, he had given all his protagonists the language of their particular temperaments and conditions. Did his heroes tend to expatiate overlong upon their moods? Well, that was a specifically Russian failing. And then, it was all clothed in such a light, fine style. No, he had not let his homeland down. And yet he considered himself Tolstoy's inferior. In him this was not humility but the product of honesty and clear sight. But he could unsheathe his claws when he wanted to: he had told the writer Saltykov-Shchedrin that the novels of Zola and Edmond de Goncourt "do not tread the path of truth and invent far too much. Their literature reeks of literature." In the same letter he had said, about Dostoyevsky's *A Raw Youth*, "I have glanced into that chaos. Lord, what a sour pottage, what a hospital stench, what stutters and stammers that nobody needs, what psychological nail-parings!"[23]

Early in 1879 he received sad news. His older brother, Nicholas,

*Pugachev was a Cossack chieftain who fomented a vast peasant uprising during the reign of Catherine II; Stenka Razin was the hero of the peasant revolt of 1667 to 1670.

had died, on January 7. They were bound together emotionally by memories of youth, the years of their struggle against their tyrannical mother. But with time their friendship had cooled. After escaping from his mother's domination, Nicholas had fallen under that of his wife, Anna Yakovlevna, as Ivan had under that of Pauline Viardot. Both were women of strong character and fiery temperament. Both were, perhaps, substitutes for the redoubtable Varvara Petrovna of their childhood. Anna Yakovlevna had died before her husband. With Nicholas gone, Turgenev suddenly felt the breath of the void blowing straight down his neck. He had another painful attack of gout. "It has been almost two weeks now that my gout has got me in its clutches again, and yesterday was the first time I was able to walk around my bedroom—on crutches, of course," he wrote to Flaubert. "Yesterday I also learned that my brother is dead; I am deeply grieved, because of the past, and for myself. We did not see much of each other and had virtually nothing in common . . . But a brother, although sometimes less, is also more than a friend. The tie can be less strong, but more intimate. My brother died a millionaire but has left his whole fortune to his wife's family. He put me down (or so he wrote me) for two hundred and fifty thousand francs in his will (that is, about the twentieth part of his fortune) but as the people he has been associating with in the last years of his life are all swindlers and crooks, I shall probably have to hurry off to deal with things myself, or my brother's bequest may very well go up in smoke."[24]

A month later he reluctantly set out for a Russia in which he was anticipating nothing but major financial reverses and minor literary letdowns.

13

THE LION

The moment he got to Moscow, Turgenev was invited to a dinner given in his honor by Maxim Kovalevsky, editor-in-chief of the *Critical Review.* A score of contributors gathered around the table. The master of the house proposed the first toast, referring to his illustrious guest as the "affectionate and indulgent guide of youth." Turgenev was stunned. Until that moment, he had supposed that the new generation felt nothing but contempt for his work, and here was somebody talking about his influence on the Russia of tomorrow. More speeches followed, alluding to the high standing of the author of *Smoke* in the nation's literature. At dinners *chez* Voisin or at the Véfour he had listened to the praises of his French friends with keen pleasure; but this time it was his fellow countrymen who were congratulating him, and on Russian soil, and in the Russian language. His eyes brimmed with tears.

Back in his rooms, he tried to bring himself to his senses by telling himself that such an about-face of public opinion was impossible and that Maxim Kovalevsky was just being nice to him. But the ensuing days confirmed this sense of a long-delayed triumph. On February 18, 1879, when he entered the amphitheater in which the Society of Friends of Russian Literature was holding its assembly, he was greeted by a long ovation. An intense young man named Victorov addressed him on behalf of those present: "A short while ago the young professors honored you. Please permit us now to honor you in turn, we young students of Russia; permit us to honor in you the author of *Memoirs of a Sportsman,* the publication of which cannot be dissociated from the emancipation of the serfs!" Turgenev was deeply touched and uttered a few modest words of thanks. Their simplicity produced a roar of enthusiasm from the audience. The students plunged down the steps pushing and shoving, smothering Turgenev with their hugs, deafening him with their cheers. A crowd of vociferous admirers accompanied him home again. "Three days ago," he wrote to Toporov, "at a meeting of the Friends of Russian Literature, the students gave me so extraordinary a reception that it left me in a daze— applause lasting five minutes, a speech from the top of the gallery, etc. The Assembly elected me an honorary member. I was overjoyed by this return of the younger generation, but also deeply shaken."[1] At times, it seemed to him as if Russia were repenting for having ignored and spurned him all these years and that he was at last about to reap some reward for his efforts. In reality, this sudden surge of popularity corresponded to a swing in the feelings of young Russian intellectuals. For a time, the idea of revolution had appealed to them, but many now found they could no longer condone the acts of the terrorists and were frightened by their fanaticism. After sneering at Turgenev, they now saw him as the exponent of a noble liberal tradition, a man of moderation and generosity of heart. He was in favor of a constitution, he condemned both the lawless attacks upon authority and the merciless counterattacks of that same authority, he was unstinting in his efforts on behalf of political exiles, he longed to see a just government in Russia, based on the people's participation in affairs of state. All of which corresponded to the aspirations of the majority of the educated citizenry. And then, the simple act of publishing one fine book after another, however unkindly they may have been greeted by the critics, had made him, unknown to himself, a classic. Some of his books—*Memoirs of a Sportsman, A Nest of Gentlefolk, Rudin, Fathers and Sons, Smoke*—had worked their way deep into the nation's collective memory.

Now, the apartment in which he was living was besieged by callers: students, actors, members of the English Club, pupils at the conservatory . . . They all arrived with flattering words and requests for autographs, and among them were a goodly number of breathless young women who identified with his heroines. In response to this groundswell of interest he attended, on March 4, a concert for needy students. There were fresh ovations, another welcoming address. The young speaker congratulated him for having been one of the first to "develop a deep feeling for the downtrodden." He replied, "For an aging writer, one who is already preparing to cease all activity, sympathy expressed in this way is, let me say very frankly, the highest and the only reward, after which he can have nothing more to hope for. It shows him that his life has not been lived in vain, that his work has not been lost, that the seed he sowed has borne fruit."

On March 8, happy and exhausted, he set out for St. Petersburg, where more banquets, speeches, and gatherings of admirers awaited him. Young ladies gushed at him over *Virgin Soil,* when less than two years before they would undoubtedly have cursed the book as being "anti-youth." He refused nothing, answered every toast, autographed every book, read passages from his works at charity benefits. "The readings, ovations, and so on continue in series, here as in Moscow," he wrote to Lyubov Stechkina.* "But, *entre nous,* however much joy I derive from them all, I shall breathe easier when it is over and I am back in the quiet of my own nest."[2]

In St. Petersburg, the Alexandrinsky Theatre was producing his old play *A Month in the Country,* at the instigation of a young actress named Marya Gavrilovna Savina, who was playing Verochka. Turgenev was worried about it. Was this the moment to bring this youthful effort before the public? With the deep inner eddies of its characters—the heroine Natalya Petrovna, obsessed by her fear of her father, or the innocent and fragile Verochka, shattered by other people's indifference, or the irresistibly charming student Belyaev, or the alarming Dr. Spigelsky who observes masters and servants with equal coolness and foretells the awakening of the proletariat—the great virtue of the play, although somewhat weighted down by their lengthy monologues, lies in the unconscious drives and yearnings of its characters and the atmosphere of old-fashioned enchantment in which the action is enveloped.

When Marya Savina learned that Turgenev was in the capital, she was both thrilled and intimidated. What would he think of her interpretation? With pounding heart, she went to call on him in his rooms in the hôtel de l'Europe. The woman he saw in the doorway was small and young, twenty-five, with sharp features and quick movements, and with his very first glance his soul quaked within him. She, meanwhile, was captivated by the silver-crested old man who was treating

*Lyubov Stechkina was a tubercular woman writer whose early works Turgenev had encouraged.

her like a child. "He was such a likable and elegant granddaddy," she wrote, "that I immediately felt quite at ease and, forgetting my awe of 'Turgenev,' started to talk like an ordinary human being."[3] She invited him to a performance of the play, and on May 15 he sat down at the back of the director's box and watched with great delight. Most of the actors he thought first rate, but Marya Savina was so natural, so sensitive, that she rose head and shoulders above them all. After the second act a few members of the audience, having recognized Turgenev in the shadows at the back of the box, began calling for the author. Marya Savina hurried offstage and returned, dragging by the hand a dazed, benumbed man who bowed to the house, smiling and choking back his tears. Before him was a horde of strangers, all clapping and bawling his name. During the intermission he went to see Marya Savina in her dressing room, grasped both her hands in his, stared at her intently in the light of the gas lamp and muttered, musing, "Verochka. Can I have written this Verochka? I never paid much attention to her; for me the important character was Natalya Petrovna. You are the living Verochka. What talent you have!" Looking at this pretty actress backstage in a theater, he was feeling the same emotion he had felt so many years before with Pauline Viardot, in the days when he sat on paw number three of the big white bearskin. The lights, the smell of greasepaint, the bustle and hurry, laughter, youth—everything here was as entrancing now as then. Surrounded by so much youthful energy, he found himself forgetting his years. The next day he agreed to appear with Marya Savina at a Literary Fund soirée. They were to read a scene from his comedy *A Provincial Lady*. Turgenev read badly, almost unintelligibly, but he was a great success even so. At the end, the author received thunderous rounds of applause. That same evening he gave a photograph of himself to Marya Savina with the inscription "In memory of our reading, Your devoted I. Turgenev."

When Pauline Viardot heard about her great friend's triumphs, she began to worry. Those Russians, if they flattered him enough, might just manage to keep Turgenev, and she needed him at her side to make her "household" complete. "Are you sure you're not going to abandon us?" she wrote on March 13, 1879. "You'll be bored in Paris if there is no longer such a fever of admiration around you . . . You will never have strength to tear yourself away from all those young people prancing and snorting around you." But there was no power on earth that could keep Turgenev in Russia.

When he left for France, on March 21, 1879, he carried in his heart a sense that he had by some miracle recovered the esteem of his fellow countrymen and the feeling that he was in the throes of a new and tender passion for a woman, Marya Savina.

His friends in Paris found him younger and in better spirits as a result of his success. But although he felt personally reconciled to Russia again, the violent events taking place there were upsetting him more and more. When he learned that the populist revolutionary Solovyev had tried to assassinate the tsar on April 2, he feared that the authorities would use this isolated act as an excuse for abandoning all plans for reform. "I am absolutely appalled by this awful news," he wrote to Polonsky. "I can foresee that some people are going to take advantage of this insane attack and use it to the detriment of the very party which, by virtue of its liberal convictions, is most deeply attached to the tsar's life and is looking to him alone to carry out reforms. For us Russians, any reform that did not come from the top would be inconceivable . . . Our one hope lies in the serenity and wisdom of the emperor himself. I am greatly vexed and tormented by all this . . . I have not slept the last two nights. I mull and ponder and get nowhere."[4]

Meanwhile, his reputation kept growing, even abroad. Oxford University awarded him an honorary doctorate, and he went to England to receive it. "There were nine of us doctors in scarlet robes, with square hats on our heads," he wrote to Annenkov. "There was a huge crowd—many ladies in particular—in the hall crowned by a cupola in which the ceremonies take place . . . I cannot speak too highly of the friendly treatment I was given by the English."[5] Later, he told Maslov, in a letter accompanying a photograph, "This scholarly headgear could hardly be less becoming to my Great Russian mug."[6]

The French made him an officer of the Order of Education, which he found rather droll: "It appears that this honor entitles you to wear a lavender ribbon—lavender, not red," he wrote to Flaubert's niece Caroline Commanville. "I shall pin it to my Oxford doctor's gown, which is bright scarlet, the two colors will go together perfectly."[7]

All these honors took his mind off his real problem, which was the absence of creative impetus. He was still writing his light little prose poems and correcting the text of an edition of his complete works. "I have gone completely stale," he told Annenkov. "My pen will do nothing that I ask of it and my brain tires terribly quickly."[8] To Wolff, "I have given up all literary activity and almost forgotten how to hold a pen."[9] Then, to his friend Pietsch: "I've been asked for something new and I do not have anything new, or anything old either. God be praised, I have stopped writing."[10]

On the other hand, he was reading a lot, and his literary judgments were as peremptory as ever. He feared that Tolstoy was "too simple and true" to please the French. Daudet's latest novel, *Les Rois en exil,* he found tolerable although weaker than its predecessors. But in spite of his friendship for its author, he thought Zola's *Nana* a terrible book. "I do not believe I have ever read anything as perfectly boring as *Nana* (keep this to yourself)," he wrote to Flaubert. "So deadly pedestrian, so plodding and pedantic, and the one or two obscenities in it, like rare seeds of poetry, are not enough to give any zest to the overall blandness of this porridge."[11] He also kept abreast of everything that was being published in Russia, including subversive pamphlets. On principle, he was hostile to the terrorists, but that did not prevent him from doing everything he could to soften the fate reserved for those who were arrested. The Russian authorities were made uneasy by this ambivalent attitude, and saw him as "flirting" with the extremists at the same time as he was scandalized by their misdeeds.

In October 1879 he wrote a prefatory letter to a French translation of a story by the revolutionary Pavlovsky, who had recently escaped from Russia. It was called "In the Cell. Impressions of a nihilist." In his presentation, Turgenev pointed out that he did not share the author's views but thought that what he related was a moving human experience. "Without in any degree approving his opinions," he wrote, "I considered that the naïve and frank narration of what he has had to suffer might, while arousing interest in the man himself, serve to prove how little justification there can be, in a sound legislation, for preventive detention in a prison cell." This explanation was printed in the Paris newspaper *Le Temps* on November 12, 1879. The moment people in Russia got wind of it, there was a great hue and cry. Conservatives saw it as encouragement to the criminal practices of the nihilists, while liberals accused Turgenev of prostituting himself to curry favor with the revolutionary young. Taken aback by the violence of these reactions, he tried to justify himself in letters to friends and editors of Russian papers. But nobody could understand how he could carry tolerance to the point of excusing, as a man, acts that, as a citizen, he must condemn. A few weeks later he gave further proof of his unreliability by recommending to Zola, for publication in the periodical *Voltaire,* a novel entitled *Victims of the Tsar,* by the revolutionary Ashkinazy. This novel was fiercely opposed to the imperial regime, and it also was not in harmony with Turgenev's moderate convictions; but, as he explained to its author, he was supporting it out of intellectual integrity. "I do not approve of the general slant of your work," he wrote. "But since I am an old liberal—and not in words alone—I respect other people's opinions even when they are contrary to my own. Not only do I not claim the right to oppose their expression; I also see no reason to avoid or prevent their public affirmation, especially in the case of a work of literature . . . I do not belong to the school that believes that the truth must be smothered; on the contrary, it must be revealed. That is why I am prepared to promote the publication of a work written by a revolutionary."[12] Prince Orlov, the Russian ambassador to France, made it known to Turgenev that the authorities took a very dim view of his concern for the maniacs who had perpetrated the assassination attempt. This was unfortunate, because Turgenev was just planning to return to Russia for a long visit. "Not to work—that, never!" he wrote to Flaubert, "but simply to breathe my native air."[13] However, it took him until the end of January 1880 to make up his mind.

Before departing, he invited his friends Zola, the Goncourts, and Daudet to a farewell dinner at the café Riché. "He is leaving for his country, this time in response to a rather strange sense of drifting and uncertainty," Edmond de Goncourt wrote in his diary.[14] During the meal Turgenev told his guests that his heart had started to behave peculiarly one night when he was lying in bed half awake, and he had distinctly seen a brown spot on the wall, which is a sure sign of death. The remainder of the evening was positively macabre, with each person discoursing upon his ailments and premonitions.

Three days later, filled with apprehensions, Turgenev left Paris for St. Petersburg. There, a long attack of gout prevented him from meeting all the friends he wanted to see, and especially Marya Savina. The town was feverishly preparing for the forthcoming inauguration of a monument to Pushkin. As usual, the intellectuals were split into two camps. The Westerners hailed Pushkin as a great European. The Slavophiles claimed that his sources were pure Russian.

As a continuer of the Pushkin tradition, Turgenev was naturally asked to speak at the ceremonies. All the most famous authors of the day were on the program—Turgenev, Tolstoy, Dostoyevsky, Goncharov, Pisemsky, Fet, Aksakov, Maykov, Grigorovich, Polonsky, Ostrovsky, Kovalevsky. By unanimous consent, Turgenev was designated leader of the Westerners and Dostoyevsky chief of the Slavophiles. Once again they were being stood face to face like irreconcilable foes.

And what was Tolstoy going to do?[15] For the moment, he had not agreed to appear. In the public mind Tolstoy, Dostoyevsky, and Turgenev formed a sort of holy trinity illuminating the whole of Russian literature. All three ought by rights to be in Moscow to commemorate their great precursor. Turgenev went to Yasnaya Polyana to try to persuade Tolstoy to come.

Tolstoy received him cordially and immediately dragged him off to shoot. He even posted his guest in the best hide, where the snipe were almost always sure to pass. But none came. Turgenev peered mournfully up at the empty sky. Sonya Tolstoy, who had accompanied him, made bold to ask why he was not writing any more. He smiled sadly and murmured, "There is no one to hear us so I shall tell you. I can't write any more. In the past, every time the desire to write took hold of me I would shiver as in a real fever of love. Now it's over. I'm old and can no longer either write or love." Just then a shot rang out and Tolstoy, hidden in the bushes, ordered his dog to retrieve the bird he had just brought down. "There he goes, he's started," said Turgenev. "Leo Nikolayevich is already at work. Now there's a happy man! All his life luck has smiled upon him."[16] And indeed the snipe were all flying Tolstoy's way. Turgenev shot only one bird the whole day, and that one caught on a branch and was not found until the next day.

Afterward, the two writers withdrew to an isba*that had been made into a study not far from the house, and Turgenev began urging Tolstoy to speak at the Pushkin ceremonies. Tolstoy's response was a firm refusal. He could not abide official ceremonies, he maintained, but Turgenev sensed his unwillingness to appear in Moscow and be seen to be competing with himself and Dostoyevsky. Stiff with pride, the author of *War and Peace* would not risk being less praised and fussed over than his colleagues. Having talked himself out of arguments, Turgenev repacked his bags and left, his mission a failure.

Alone at Spasskoye, he struggled painfully to compose his speech on Pushkin. In the middle of writing it, he read in a newspaper that Flaubert was dead. The news shook him enough to kill all desire to write for some hours. "I heard about it in the most brutal way possible," he told Zola. "I don't need to tell you how grieved I am.

*A log hut/cabin.

Flaubert was one of the men I cared most about in all the world. It is not just a great talent that we are losing; it is a special, unique person, and a focal point for all of us."[17] And to Caroline Commanville, "Your uncle's death is one of the greatest sorrows of my whole life and I cannot get used to the thought that I shall never see him again . . . This is one of those sorrows one does not *want* to get over."[18]

Nevertheless, he finished his speech and, shaking off his gloom, let his thoughts return to the radiant memory of Marya Savina. For her birthday he had given the young woman a little gold bracelet with their two names engraved on the inside. He thought of her, in his solitude at Spasskoye, as his last chance of love. Twenty-five and sixty-two were their ages: there was a century between them. All he could hope for from her was a breath of fresh air. In real life he belonged to Pauline Viardot, in his dreams to Marya Savina. He asked only that she let him go on dreaming as long as possible. He was both tormented and fulfilled by this role as poetic swain. "I feel now," he wrote her, "that I love you sincerely. I feel that you have become something in my life from which I shall never be parted."[19] He invited her to Spasskoye, but she refused—she had to go to Odessa for a season of performances. Her itinerary took her by way of Mtsensk and Orel. On May 6, 1880, Turgenev, quaking like a callow youth, went to the little station of Mtsensk to wait for the train that was carrying the young woman. It stopped a few minutes in the night. Turgenev quickly climbed aboard. Facing him, the beloved face broadened into a smile. He sat with Marya Savina in her compartment as far as Orel, gazing at her, inhaling her, kissing her hands. At Orel they had to part. At the last minute, already on the platform, he was sorry he hadn't kissed her. He hadn't dared to. His age, the shame and ridicule of it. She sat at the window waving her handkerchief. His heart was heavy. This impossible love was a mockery of fate.

The next day, back at Spasskoye, he wrote to her. "Dear Marya Gavrilovna, I have been back an hour and a half and already I am writing to you. I spent the night at Orel—an excellent night, because I never stopped thinking of you, a bad night because I was unable to close my eyes . . . If you were here, we should be sitting on the terrace at this moment, admiring the scene, I should talk to you of various unimportant things and, in thought, in a rush of gratitude, I should constantly be kissing your little feet . . . when, yesterday evening, you sat by the open window and I, speechless across from you, suddenly uttered the word 'madness'; you attributed it to yourself, but I had something different in mind. I was tempted by an idea that truly was madness—the idea of seizing you and carrying you off to the station . . . Unfortunately, prudence prevailed. The bell rang and *ciao,* as the Italians say. Just think what the newspapers would have said! I can see the story, headed 'Scandal at the Orel railway station.' 'An extraordinary event took place here yesterday: the author T . . . , an elderly man, was accompanying the celebrated actress S . . . , who was traveling to Odessa for a brilliant season in the theater there, when, just as the train was about to pull out, he, as though possessed by the devil in person, extracted Madame S . . . through the window of her compartment and, overcoming the artiste's desperate efforts, etc. etc.' What thunder and upheavals there would be all over Russia! And yet it very nearly happened, as is almost always the case in life."[20]

Two days later, in another letter to Marya Savina, he confessed that even while he was drafting his Pushkin speech, in the depths of his soul "there was echoing a single, same note." All of a sudden," he wrote, "I find my lips murmuring, 'What a night we should have spent! And what would have happened the next morning? God alone knows!' You are wrong to reproach yourself with anything, saying that I am your 'sin.' Alas, that I shall never be. And if we meet again in another two or three years, I shall be an old, old man. As for you, you will have entered definitively upon the normal course of your life and nothing will remain of our past . . . Your whole life is in front of you, mine is behind, and that hour in the train, when I felt myself almost a young fellow of twenty again, was the last flicker of the lamp. It is hard for me to explain to myself the feeling you have aroused in me. I do not know if I am in love with you. In the past it was different. There is that indefinable need for fusion and possession and the giving of oneself, in which sensitivity itself vanishes in a sort of delicate flame . . . I am talking nonsense, no doubt, but I should have been unspeakably happy if, if . . . Knowing now that it will not be, I am not exactly what one could call unhappy, I do not even feel melancholy, but I am profoundly regretful that that wonderful night should be lost forever without having even brushed me with the tip of its wing. I regret it for myself and—I make bold to say—for you, for I am convinced that you would not forget the happiness you would have given me. I should not be writing this to you if I did not feel that this is a farewell letter. Our correspondence will not cease, of course. Oh, no! I hope we shall often tell each other what is happening to us, but that half-open door, that door through which something mysteriously wonderful could be glimpsed, has swung shut for good. That's exactly it, the bolt is shot.

Whatever happens, I shall never be the same, and nor shall you." Turgenev added a postscript, "Please, do not be fearful for the future, you will never get another letter like this."[21]

While he was writing these agonizing lines, Marya Savina was preparing to meet, in Odessa, a brilliant officer of hussars named Nikita Vsevolozhsky, who was courting her insistently. To her, Turgenev was the intellectual friend, Vsevolozhsky a promise of marriage with a man who was young, rich, handsome, and highly regarded. Instinctively, the old writer was carrying on in real life like some of the heroes of his novels—full of impulses, indecisiveness, and sorrow. Love, in his heart, was synonymous with defeat; a defeat one could not forgo.

It took a great effort of will to put aside these thoughts of Marya Savina and return to his obligations as an author, but the date for the Pushkin festivities was drawing near, and so he dutifully betook himself and his melancholy to Moscow. The moment he got there, he plunged into a great literary maëlstrom. The antagonism between Westerners and Slavophiles had reached such a pitch that it was causing feuds within families. The Slavophiles were backing Dostoyevsky as the prime exponent of the nation's traditional virtues, while the Westerners, closing up ranks behind Turgenev, were busily organizing their leader's triumph, recruiting volunteers for his claque, issuing carefully calculated invitations.

On the morning of June 6, 1880, the delegates of the Russian writers laid their wreaths at the foot of the Pushkin monument. Turgenev was deeply moved as he performed this symbolic gesture. He had known Pushkin alive and seen him dead in his coffin, he carried on his person a lock of the poet's hair, he thought of himself as his emulator. A short while later, at a meeting at Moscow University, the rector announced that Turgenev had been made an honorary member of the institution. The students in the hall acclaimed the old novelist loudly, while he bowed his head in acknowledgment of their applause. Then came the inevitable banquet at the Assembly of Nobility. Every toast contained some allusion to Pushkin, but the proposers were not in unison. Each had a different notion of Pushkin's significance to the fatherland. Was he specifically Russian or comprehensively European? Katkov, a hotheaded Slavophile who had attacked Turgenev in his review, raised his glass to a reconciliation; but Turgenev would not drink with a spokesman for government reactionism. That evening, from a platform, he read one of Pushkin's poems. His weary, haggard, handsome face, his white crest of hair, his quavering voice, earned him an ovation. Dostoyevsky, who followed him, was also highly applauded. "But," he wrote to his wife, "Turgenev, who read very badly, was called back more times than I."

The official ceremony of the Society of Friends of Russian Literature took place on June 7, again at the Assembly of Nobility. Turgenev got up to speak to an audience that was, on the whole, favorable to him. They sat with their eyes fixed upon the elegant, massive giant, expecting him, through his praises of Pushkin, to send them into raptures of patriotism. Instead, he pronounced the most carefully measured, moderate speech imaginable. He paid tribute to Pushkin's boundless talent but was not certain that this was the author who should be seen as personifying the specific genius of his race. "Can we confer upon him the title of national poet, in the same way as the English can Shakespeare, the Germans can Goethe, and one or two others?" Turgenev asked. "Let us leave that question to one side for the moment. There is no doubt, at any rate, that he has created our language of poetry, our literary language, and that all that remains for us, for us and our descendants, is to walk upon the trail broken by his genius." The listeners were a little disappointed by so much reasonableness, but they applauded heartily all the same.

This undeserved success made Dostoyevsky angry. The Pushkin commemoration was turning increasingly into a duel between two ideas, two men: on one side the cultivated, controlled, liberal, skeptical European, and on the other the integral Russian, the wild-eyed, nationalist visionary.

The next day, June 8, it was Dostoyevsky's turn to dazzle the masses. He stood before his audience, wan and ailing, shaggily untidy, twitching and jerking, his voice rasping. But with his very first words he had the hall eating out of his hand. With breathless conviction he claimed that Pushkin embodied the national genius in its ability to comprehend and assimilate those of other nations. Pushkin represented the universal side of Russia, and the Russia he had so beautifully celebrated was destined to lead the world down the path to moral perfection. The regeneration of Europe would come from her because she alone had kept the pure faith of the early Christians. Little by little, his speech was turning into a sermon, his literary analysis into prophecy. Every step in the progress of the speaker's messianic demonstration was greeted by a roar from the galvanized crowd. When, at length, he fell silent, exhausted and hoarse, a furor broke out. The audience clapped, shouted, sobbed. Enemies embraced, swearing to bury their long-lived feuds. Young ladies climbed onto the platform to kiss the great man's hands. One group of ecstatic females wove a laurel wreath and placed it on his brow. Turgenev got a wreath too, but he knew the battle was lost. What was he doing there? However deeply he loved his homeland, patriotic fervor of any description made him shudder. He knew Europe far too well to be blind where Russia's merits were concerned. His moderation in art and politics, no doubt, was not in harmony with the tastes of the mob. His countrymen were avid for sublimity and emotional raptures; they could not identify with him. Tolstoy had been shrewder; he had been right to decline the invitation, so as not to have to witness this deification of Dostoyevsky. "At your request," Turgenev wrote to Marya Savina, "I enclose the text of my speech. I do not know if it will interest you. Its effect upon the public was slight."[22]

At the end of June 1880 he left, weary and disenchanted, for France. How much longer would he have the strength to go on shuttling back and forth between these two countries that were fighting for his heart?

14

PRESENTIMENTS

Paris again, Bougival, the Viardot family, the French friends. Flaubert's absence cast a pall over their habitual restaurant reunions. "We missed his strong voice and his bellows of laughter,"[1] wrote Alphonse Daudet. Turgenev gladly agreed to act as vice-chairman of the committee set up to commission a statue in Flaubert's honor and even solicited contributions from Russia. His compatriots found this distasteful: the newspapers said it was ridiculous, readers sputtered that he was begging money to promote the fame of a foreigner. He received many anonymous letters. "Insulting articles in all the papers and a storm of anonymous letters have proven to me that in turning to the people of Russia to request a token contribution for the monument to my friend Flaubert I was making a foolish mistake," he wrote to Polonsky. "Heaven is my witness that I shall not put their money into my own pocket, which certain of my correspondents' allusions seem to imply."[2] A few weeks later, also to Polonsky, "Anonymous letters filled with insults are still arriving . . . In the latest, I am called a renegade, an imbecile, and a prostitute. And all on account of Flaubert!"[3]

As Turgenev was writing this letter, Dostoyevsky lay dying in St. Petersburg. The bombshell fell on January 28, 1881: the author was no more. His great rival's disappearance left Turgenev with mixed feelings of vindication and mourning. He had cared for neither the writer nor the man. Dostoyevsky's novels bored him. He considered his apocalyptic teachings both pernicious and grotesque. And yet he could not deny that this chaotic, antiartistic, half-demented body of work had left its mark upon the sensitivity of the Russian public. It could not have been more unlike his own work, which was all in subtle halftones, twists and turns, nostalgia. Whether he liked it or not, there was now a Dostoyevskian universe and a Dostoyevskian philosophy to reckon with, even if one disagreed with them. He reluctantly consented to write an obituary for the *European Messenger* in honor of this colleague whom he had hated during his lifetime, and another for Pisemsky, who had died a few days before him; but he quickly abandoned the thankless task. "What they want from me," he told Pypin, an editor at the *European Messenger,* "is an assessment of the work of the two deceased writers, and not literary reminiscences of my relations with them. It is very hard for me to do this, in the first place, and in the second place I am afraid that the readers, in their present mood, will inevitably feel that I have once again snatched at an opportunity to put myself to the fore, to impose myself."[4]

A second refusal: he would not attend the giant demonstration that was to take place outside Victor Hugo's house on February 16, 1881, when the poet entered his eightieth year. The reason he gave was an attack of gout; but the truth was that he did not want to be involved in a public homage that he considered excessive and senseless. "Even had I been well," he wrote to Stasulevich, "I should not have gone. Let the French mollycoddle their idol if they like, but what is the point of it for us?"[5] His views of Hugo as novelist had been expressed on many occasions, in particular to Adelaide Lukanina, who had met him in Paris: "*Les Miserables* is nothing but falsehood. From start to finish, every word of it is untrue, everything is fake! . . . You would not find that in our literature. Our intentions are simple, we are often boring but we never depart from real life, as the French do." And in support of his opinion he quoted a phrase of the short story master, Mérimée: "Russian art will achieve beauty through the force of truth."[6] Similarly, he urged Stasulevich to read Maupassant: "Out of the whole school of young writers in France, the one with the most talent is Guy de Maupassant, who wrote '*Boule de Suif.*' "[7]

Into these mundane preoccupations dropped a thunderbolt: the assassination of Tsar Alexander II, dismembered by a bomb on March 1, 1881, on his way back from a military inspection. To Turgenev, the loss of this ruler, who had freed the serfs and promised the country a constitution, was the deathblow to all liberals. The terrorists who had slain the emperor in the street, in broad daylight, were in his opinion monsters of stupidity and irresponsibility, and no thinking person could condone their act. By immolating the most broadminded monarch ever to rule over Russia, they were injuring the cause of the revolution and positively encouraging the authorities to increase their control over the movements of all people hoping for change. "And what will happen if attacks are made upon the new tsar [Alexander III]?" he wrote to Annenkov. "If that occurs, all that will be left us is to cover our eyes and run away to the ends of the earth, until the muzhik's noose begins to tighten around your civilized epiglottis."[8] He elaborated upon his ideas in an article on the new emperor that he wrote in French and published in the *Revue politique et littéraire:* "As for the nihilists, who imagine that the emperor can be driven by fear to grant further concessions, and even to give the country a constitution: they are grossly mistaken, having no notion of his strength of character and energy. All that their attempts at intimidation will accomplish is to dam up the liberal current that is natural to him; if he swims a few strokes in that direction it will not be because they have intimidated him, but in spite of their threats to him."

This was his mood as he made preparations to return to Russia once again. But before setting out he was a joyful guest at the wedding of Pauline Viardot's youngest daughter, Marianne, to a young composer named Alphonse Duvernoy. "They will surely have a happy marriage," he wrote to Marya Savina, "because they love each other sincerely and their personalities could not be better matched. I need hardly tell you how happy I am for them, although I do feel an emptiness in the house."[9] He promised that he would soon be seeing her in Russia again, and set out on April 26/May 8, 1881. Throughout his latest stay in France he had carried on a well-bred exchange of letters with Marya Savina, worrying about her health, applauding her successes in the theater, harking back to their last meetings and "kissing every little finger of [her] right hand." Upon reaching Spasskoye he braved himself to renew his invitation to the young woman to visit him there and, oh wonder! she accepted. He also invited his old friends the Polonskys. For four days Marya Savina's youth and laughter gave new life to the house. She bathed in the pond, far from indiscreet eyes. There was lunch on the terrace, then Turgenev retired to work in his study. He was putting the finishing touches to a fantasy he had started at Bougival in 1879, "The Song of Love Triumphant." In the evening he went out onto the balcony with Marya Savina, listened to "the voices of the night," inhaled the odors of the drowsing countryside, questioned the actress about her love life. Their conversations, continuing far into the night, left him with a sense of sweet bitterness, of helpless loss. On July 17, the Polonskys' wedding anniversary, he arranged an elegant dinner, served champagne, made a little congratulatory speech, and invited seventy peasant boys and girls to sing and dance their wild country dances for his guests. With shining eyes, Marya Savina nodded in time and hummed the refrains along with the chorus. "It's the gypsy blood in her coming out!" said Turgenev. He himself danced a few ponderous steps while the Polonskys strummed on the piano, and then summoned his houseguests into his study where he read them "The Song of Love Triumphant." It is a long short story, dedicated to Flaubert. The action takes place in Ferrara, Italy, in the sixteenth century. Two men, a painter and a musician, are in love with the same woman, Valery. The painter marries her. The musician leaves for the Far East and returns four years later accompanied by a mute Malaysian. In the interval he has learned sorcery, and, by virtue of the magic powers acquired in foreign lands, he takes possession of Valery's soul. He invades her dreams and she, unconscious and bewitched, gives herself to him. Then he takes her twice, by night, to the pavilion where he lives. Both times, before leaving her, he plays "The Song of Love Triumphant" on his violin. The whole story, invented by Turgenev, is steeped in the supernatural and full of dreams and hypnotism. The contrast between the author's clear, cool style and the eerie twists of his tale is striking. Beyond any doubt, the inspiration for this work came from his impossible love for Marya Savina. Since she would not yield to him in real life, he could at least possess her in his dreams, like the Italian musician. He would have given so much to be able to bewitch the young woman with his hero's mysterious recipe! Did Marya Savina guess the underlying meaning of the story Turgenev was reading to her? She said it was wonderful, at any rate, and the Polonskys were also lavish in their praise. Turgenev purred; but he also feared the reaction of the press, and he was right. Apart from one or two periodicals that praised the author's purity of language, the rest rejected the tale as too farfetched. Turgenev would have liked Marya Savina to stay longer at Spasskoye but she left the day after the reading, and soon after announced her engagement to Nikita Vsevolozhsky.

Turgenev subsided into gloom and apathy. His mind was perpetually dwelling on death. Hearing that there was a cholera epidemic at Bryansk, he was instantly convinced that he had every symptom of the disease, though Bryansk was three hundred versts from Spasskoye and Turgenev was plainly in very good health. To Polonsky, who pointed out this fact to him, he said, "The thought has come into my head, the word has sat on my tongue, and that's the end of it . . . The thought that cholera will take me from one minute to the next never leaves my mind. Whatever else I am thinking, whatever I may say, even if I seem quite unconcerned, inside my brain the same thing is spinning round and round, cholera, cholera, cholera . . . Like a madman, I have even given it a physiognomy. I see it as a rotting, stinking, greenish-yellow old woman . . . When there was a cholera epidemic in Paris I could smell it: it smelled of damp and mushrooms and long-unused toilets. And I'm afraid, afraid, afraid . . ."

As the Polonskys were getting ready for bed one night, he came to their room looking as if he had seen a ghost and saying that a mysterious bird was beating at his windowpane. Mrs. Polonsky followed him to his study and opened the casement. She cradled the bird in her hands; it was smaller than a sparrow and its black eyes were terrified. She put it in a cage and Turgenev mournfully observed, when she let it out the next morning, "It flew away to freedom and some sparrow hawk will sink its talons into it and eat it."

This bird beating against his window in the night seemed to him to be bearing some ominous message. He had taken it into his head, heaven knows why, that he would die on October 2, 1881, and he told Polonsky, "Not for anything in the world could I bear to be buried in the family vault in our cemetery here at Spasskoye. I went there once and I shall never forget the horrifying impression I came away with: damp, mold, cobwebs, sowbugs, stale tomb air, brrr!"

Pauline Viardot wrote that a poisonous insect had stung her in the face, and this threw him into such a terror that Polonsky and his wife had great difficulty bringing him to his senses. Pauline's nose had swollen, she was in bed. "It's extremely dangerous," Turgenev kept saying. "I ought to go to France." "Would you just drop everything, and Spasskoye, and us, and your work, and go off?" Polonsky asked him. "Yes, I would drop everything!" Turgenev insisted.[10] Telegrams flew back and forth between Spasskoye and Bougival, and Turgenev's fears were calmed, Pauline Viardot was out of danger; so he decided to spend the rest of the summer on his estate. The room in which Marya Savina slept had become sacred. "It is and will always remain Savina's room,"[11] he wrote to the young woman. At the same time he wanted to know how definite her engagement was. "If your marriage is not to interfere with your acting career, why should those who love you, and to whom you are precious, be other than delighted by your decision?"[12] he said, although in reality this detachment, inevitable because of the difference in their ages, made him miserable. "When shall I see you again?" he asked. "And who will you be then? Mrs. Vsevolozhsky?"[13] He himself was preparing to return to France. "As for myself, although physically I am still here, in my mind I am already back there," he said in the same letter. "I can feel my French skin growing beneath my Russian skin, which is about to slough off."

On the way to St. Petersburg he stopped off at Yasnaya Polyana on August 22, 1881, to call on Tolstoy.[14] It was Sonya Tolstoy's birthday, there was a large and lively crowd of guests. Turgenev proposed a game: each person should relate the happiest moment of his or her life. When his own turn came, he smiled sadly, assumed an exalted air, and murmured, "The happiest moment of my life is, of course, a moment of love. It is that in which you meet the eyes of the woman you love and sense that she loves you too. It has happened to me once, perhaps twice."

Listening to him, it was hard for Tolstoy to hide his annoyance. Then, yielding to the pleas of the young people present, Turgenev undertook to show them how the cancan was danced in Paris. He took off his jacket and stuck his thumbs in the armholes of his waistcoat. As he jigged up and down, lifting his legs, wagging his head and panting heavily, the whole household clapped and laughed. Finally he collapsed, breathless, into an armchair. They crowded round him, plying him with questions about France. He talked about the dens of iniquity he had visited, the French authors who were friends of his. He said the realists went much too far, and from there slipped naturally into a condemnation of Dostoyevsky. "Do you know what an inverted platitude is?" he asked. "When a man is in love his heart beats wildly; when he is angry he turns scarlet, and so forth. Those are platitudes. But with Dostoyevsky everything is backwards. For example, a man meets a lion. What does he do? He turns pale, of course, and tries to run away or hide. In any ordinary story, one by Jules Verne for example, that's the way it would be. But with Dostoyevsky it's the other way around: a man sees a lion, he turns scarlet and stays put. That is what is known as an inverted platitude. It's an easy way to gain a reputation as a new, original kind of author. And then, with Dostoyevsky, on every other page his heroes are delirious or frantic or fevered. Come, now! That's not the way things happen in real life."[15] Tolstoy sat by, silently agreeing with this posthumous demolition of a celebrity that he himself considered undeserved; but he could not forgive Turgenev's trivial chatter and his grotesque clowning in front of the family. That evening he wrote in his diary, "August 22. Turgenev—cancan. Sad."

Ten days later Turgenev had reached Bougival, but was quickly driven out by the autumn damp; he removed himself to the rue de Douai in Paris, where he found the Viardots. Pauline still gave singing lessons, sang herself now and then, in a rather faded voice, played the piano, entertained friends, and kept up a steady stream of coming and going and chatter in the house. This time, however, her imperious presence was no longer enough to fill all Turgenev's thoughts. Now that he was separated from Marya Savina, she was constantly in his mind. In reality, she was a flirt who had been amusing herself, arousing the passions of this famous and vulnerable old man with her coquetry; on rare occasions she had allowed him to brush her lips with a respectful sigh, but nothing more. What was between them was an inoffensive game, which charmed them both. Although he knew she was engaged, he wrote her letters full of love and anxiety. He reminded her of "the warm and luminous kiss" she had given him one evening at dinner.[16] He frowned when he learned that Vsevolozhsky had postponed the date of the wedding on what seemed to him a very feeble pretext: "Still, *le vin est tiré, il faut le boire* [the wine is drawn and must be drunk]. After all that you have accepted or allowed to be done, there is no drawing back for you now. You are about to unite your destiny with that of a man with whom, as far as I can make out, you have very little in common. I hope in any event that you will remain free enough to continue your work on the stage."[17] He told her the mad dream that had been haunting him for days—to go to Italy with her. "Picture it to yourself: Venice, for example, in October (the best month in Italy), or Rome. Two strangers, in traveling clothes, are walking along the streets or drifting past in a gondola. One is tall and clumsy, with white hair and long legs; he is very happy. The other is a slender young woman with splendid dark eyes and black hair and she, we will suppose, is also happy. They visit the art galleries, the churches, they dine together alone, in the evening they go to the theater together and then . . . And then my imagination respectfully stops. Because there is something that must not be said? Or because there is nothing to be hushed up? . . . I'm writing too much nonsense . . . Whereupon (since nobody but yourself will read this letter), I take your charming head in my hands and kiss your lips, of that wonderful quick pink, and I tell myself that they burn and move beneath my kiss. Do I imagine . . . or do I remember?"[18]

The fact is that Marya Savina's sentimental affairs were highly complicated. She was engaged to marry Nikita Vsevolozhsky, yes, but she also felt much tender affection for Turgenev and was not insensitive to the distinguished allure of a thirty-eight-year-old general named Michael Skovelev. Turgenev complained feebly about this emotional tangle, but would have cut off his right arm sooner than give up his correspondence with the impalpable Marya Savina. She said her life in the theater had exhausted her and she was thinking of leaving the stage for a few months. Heaven forbid she should fall ill.

Turgenev's admiration for the talent of Marya Savina was equaled only by his distaste for the overacting of certain French ladies of the stage, especially Sarah Bernhardt. When he heard that the Divine Sarah was to perform in St. Petersburg he wrote to Stasulevich, "I beg of you, as a personal favor, to ask your theater critic to give Sarah Bernhardt the sharpest edge of his tongue; she is a talentless puppet, a grimacing female who has only one thing to her credit and that is her wonderful voice; all the rest is falsehood, artifice, and paltry Parisian chic."[19]

Marya Savina had been ordered to rest and was preparing to go to Italy herself. Turgenev approved of this plan, a shade sourly: "Many years ago (in 1858) I spent ten wonderful days in Florence . . . and yet I was there alone. What a gala time I would have had if I had had a pleasing, gentle, pretty (an essential quality) traveling companion. In those days I had not turned forty. A respectable age, but I still felt very young. I was not the ruin I am today . . . You are a beauty and not a beauty made of stone. But my rays do not warm you. You must have a warrior—and a young one—and an immortal. What can be done about that? You're perfectly right."[20]

At last, at the end of March 1882, Marya Savina came to Paris. Turgenev paid her a call, bearing a potted azalea, and said, "You must blossom too." He was worried. His daughter, Paulinette, was in desperate straits: after spending all her money, her husband had started to drink and was now threatening to kill her. She had been forced to run away and had sought refuge with her father. "Take your two children," he had written, "and bring them here with you. I shall find you a place to live and we shall immediately put in hand the procedure for an official separation."[21] Also, Louis Viardot was seriously ill, and Turgenev himself was suffering from acute neuralgia.

The sight of Marya Savina, however, brought him relief. Every time he found himself in her presence he felt the years drop away from him. Now more than before, she needed him. Not only did she no longer know which of her men she loved, but she was also worried about her own health. The physicians she had consulted were lost in conjecture as to the cause of her languor. Turgenev used all his connections to get her an appointment with the famous Charcot, but the medical luminary seemed more alarmed by Turgenev's condition than by that of his protégée. After examining him, he diagnosed angina pectoris and ordered him to keep to his rooms for several days.

So Marya Savina came to see him at 50, rue de Douai.* Her reaction to his life there, his clinging like some vine to the Viardot family, was one of mingled pity and jealousy. He was overpowered by the smiling authority of the "wondrous Pauline," reduced in her company to a sort of sentimental and domestic slavery. True, he was a free man in the house, he could withdraw to his rooms on the top floor, he had his own servant and was not short of money. But from morning to night his whole existence was permeated by Pauline's presence and Pauline's voice. When he was with her, he had no more will or identity of his own.

Marya Savina returned, dismayed, to Russia. She passed on her impressions to Polonsky, who told Turgenev of his own concern for the author, and Turgenev flew into a temper. "Savina is a fool," he wrote to Polonsky. "She saw only one of the four rooms at my disposal—my bedroom, no smaller or lower-ceilinged than the general run of Parisian bedrooms. Not only am I not bored by the music that surrounds me, I have even spent two hundred francs having an acoustical tube installed so that I can hear it more clearly. Viardot is very old, true, but I am not in my first youth either, and I see him once a day for a total of five minutes. As for Madame Viardot's wonderful children and Madame Viardot herself, they are constantly with me. The only thing in my life that might fairly inspire pity is my illness, which I believe to be incurable. But from every other possible point of view, I live like a king."[22]

In fact, Turgenev was obsessively worried about his health. He was naturally inclined to fear the worst and was already imagining himself doomed. "I am afflicted with a strange ailment, stupid, not dangerous but undoubtedly incurable: angina pectoris," he wrote to Annenkov. "What it means is that when the patient is prone and motionless he feels quite all right, but the moment he gets up and takes a few steps (let alone trying to climb a staircase), he is assailed by unbearable pain, first in the left shoulder, then all over the chest,

*The Viardots' town house stood at what was initially called 48, but later 50, rue de Douai.

and in the end he can no longer breathe at all. It's two weeks now since I have left my room. Charcot, whom I finally managed to see, defined my illness as a gouty cardiac neuralgia and prescribed some medicine; he warned me that 'medicine can do nothing for diseases of this kind, which wear themselves out in the end,' and when I asked him how long I should have to stay in bed he told me, with a charming smile, 'There is absolutely no way of knowing, several weeks perhaps, or perhaps several months.' "[23] To his friend Pietsch he wrote, "I am in good hands here . . . They have treated my whole shoulder with ignipuncture already, and tomorrow they are to do it again. This is all done just on principle, as there is *no* hope of a cure. As an individual, my life is over. The most I can hope for is to preserve some shadow of personality."[24]

A few days later he felt a little better and got up. "I managed to sit in a chair for fifteen minutes," he told Mrs. Polonsky, "and stood up for two minutes, which is particularly important. My gout is almost over and the pain in my shoulder and chest has diminished considerably. But four days ago I had a terrific attack of liver colic."[25] And when Mrs. Polonsky, alarmed, offered to come to Paris to stay with him, he panicked. Pauline Viardot was nursing her patient with such care and competence that she would never consent to share her responsibilities with some interloper. He could not afford to rub his "guardian angel's" ego the wrong way. He rushed off a letter to the Polonskys urging them not to make the trip: "Any idea of helping or caring for me would be out of the question. The ladies here, who are acting the part of nurses with such selflessness, would take any outside intervention as an affront. More simply, they would oppose the idea."[26] The Polonskys gave up their plan.

Meanwhile, Turgenev had received a grouchily compassionate letter from Tolstoy, typical of the style of the master of Yasnaya Polyana: "The news of your illness has caused me much sorrow, especially when I was assured that it was serious. I realized how much I cared for you. I felt that I should be much grieved if you were to die before me."[27] With rather impudent courage Turgenev wrote back, thanking him for his solicitude and adding, "As for me, I plan to live a long time yet, although I have already done singing my little refrain. But you are the one who should live many more years, and not only because, when all is said and done, life is a good thing, but in order to finish the work which it is your vocation to complete and for which we have no other master but you."[28]

The patient was complaining less of pain, so a family council was held and it was decided to take him to Bougival, where the spring, the fresh air, the view of the garden from his window, might hasten his recovery. He was delighted with the prospect of this change of scene and prepared for it by sorting all his papers. On June 6, 1882, he was loaded, "like a trunk" as he put it, into the coach. Covered in shawls, nauseous, his bones shaken by the jolting vehicle, he wondered if his strength would last the trip.

15

~~~~

HIS LAST
RETURN

Contrary to Turgenev's hopes, the country air had no effect on the progress of his illness; in fact, during the first days after their arrival at Bougival he felt even worse than before. Despite the charms of the garden glimpsed through his window, the pale new greenery, the bright clumps of flowers and innocent butterflies, he measured with terror the speed at which his disease was advancing. Dr. Jaccoud, seconded by Dr. Bertenson, had told him to drink milk. With shuddering repugnance, he struggled through twelve glasses a day. "My disease is chronic and not a single doctor can tell me how long it will last," he wrote to Pietsch. "I cannot think of traveling or working, and this may go on for years."[1] He was too weak to walk. Even sitting, he suffered from fierce intercostal pain. His nights were hellish. In his rare moments of respite he tried to take an interest in events in the world outside. He read a pamphlet on the pogroms in Russia and regretted that he was too weak to write an article on them, but expressed his sympathy for the persecuted Jews in a letter to Kolbasin: "The only way to stop these atrocities would be a strong word spoken by the tsar, which the people would hear in the churches . . . But the tsar is silent. And under the circumstances, what force is there in the voice of the intelligentsia alone? *New Time* [a reactionary paper] will spit upon you, accuse you of trying to put on airs, even intimate that you have been bought by the Jews. All one can do is blush (especially here in Europe), blush for oneself, for one's fatherland, for one's people, and be silent. I feel so unwell that I cannot write at any length. If I get better I shall let you know. Should you receive no more letters from me, know that there was once a certain writer who had been able in his day to create a little something, but that now that writer is no more and in his place there is nothing but a sick old man in a corner who not only is no longer looking ahead, he is trying not to look at what is all around him."[2]

Unable to write himself, he envied his colleagues who were imperturbably continuing their careers. Even now, ill as he was, literature remained his passion. He delivered his opinions as authoritatively as ever. Hugo's bombast irritated him more and more, and against it he held up the exemplary simplicity and truthfulness of Tolstoy. He could not understand some people's infatuation with Balzac. "I have never managed to read more than ten pages of him at a stretch, so offputting and alien do I find him,"[3] he wrote to Weinberg. On the other hand, he enthusiastically recommended Maupassant's *Une Vie* to Stasulevich: "I was literally transported. Nothing to equal it has been seen since *Madame Bovary.*"[4]

Gazing out his study window at the garden, he thought sadly of the big house waiting for him back at Spasskoye. He should have so loved to make one last pilgrimage to the scenes of his youth. At his request, the Polonskys agreed to spend the summer there. "When you are at Spasskoye," he wrote them, "give my greetings to the house, the garden, my young oak tree; greet my homeland which, no doubt, I shall never see again."[5] The Polonskys picked leaves and flowers from the garden and sent them to him by letter. The Spasskoye peasants wrote, wishing him a speedy recovery, and he replied, thanking them for their concern. "Rumors have reached me to the effect that you have been drinking much less wine of late," he added. "I am delighted to hear it and hope you will remain sober hereafter. Drunkeness is the peasant's downfall. But I am sorry to learn, according to those same rumors, that your children go so seldom to school. Remember that in our day an illiterate man is the same as a blind man or a man with only one arm."[6]

The doctors had invented a device that they fitted to his shoulder; it rested on his left collarbone. This gave him some relief; but the slightest accidental movement sent the pain in his chest rocketing through him. He could not raise his arm above his head. "Other hands," he shamefacedly confessed to Mrs. Polonsky, "must brush and comb and wash me."[7] Trying to make him more comfortable, they wrapped him in hot towels, and at night, he received a small injection of morphine. And there were the everlasting floods of milk. He was no longer living, he was surviving, and he accepted the ordeal with fatalistic courage. He was not a believer, so he looked for no solace in the prospect of an afterlife. And yet a sense of the supernatural was with him every moment of the day. Exhausted as he was, it inspired him to write an occasional prose poem, one of which he provisionally called "After Death."

In this desert of bitterness and anguish, Marya Savina's rare letters brought both regrets and consolation. "Remember, now and then, how painful it was for me to say goodbye to you in Paris, and all that I then felt," she wrote. Deeply moved, he answered: "Your letter fell into my gray existence like a rose petal on the surface of a muddy stream . . . I know as a certainty that if our two lives had come together sooner . . . But what is the good of all that? I am like my German Lemm in *A Nest of Gentlefolk,* I am looking into the tomb, not into a rose-colored tomorrow . . ."[8]

The following month Marya Savina finally made up her mind and married Nikita Vsevolozhsky. With ill-disguised irritation, Turgenev complimented her on her decision. "I congratulate you not only upon your marriage, but because you have finally found your way out of the false situation that was tormenting you," he wrote. And as she had promised to send him a plaster cast of her hand, he added, "Until then I kiss your hand, not the one in plaster but the living one, and whatever else, in your new condition, you may consent to make over to my kisses."[9]

He felt a little better in August and took advantage of the fact to finish "After Death." The story, which he later called "Clara Milich," was yet another tale of unrequited love and fatal enchantment. He based it on the true story of the singer Kadmina, with whom a zoology professor named Alenitsyn had fallen so deeply in love that he went mad, whereupon she committed suicide. Clara Milich, Turgenev's heroine, is a passionate young actress who falls in love with an icy ascetic named Aratov. Spurned by him, she poisons herself on stage. After her death, Aratov is bewitched by the magical charm of her memory. Alive, he did not love her, but he longs for her now that she is dead. She takes possession of him, comes to him at night in his dreams, maddens him with evil delights, and drives him to insanity and death.

Although unmoved by the blandishments of religion, Turgenev, like many other unbelievers, thirsted powerfully for eternity. As his strength failed, he clung more and more fiercely to the hope of another world that would not be totally severed from this one. In him, this vague notion went hand in hand with his desire for formal perfection in literature. "Clara Milich," conceived and written when its author was enduring atrocious physical sufferings, has a dazzling purity of style. Never before had Turgenev so intimately interwoven the supernatural of his subject matter with the clarity of his language. The first people to see the manuscript could hardly believe it was the work of an ailing elderly man. In the press, "Clara Milich" was qualified as a "pearl of poetry," filled with "luminous truth." Later, surprised by this response, Turgenev was to write in his diary, "My short story has been published in St. Petersburg and Moscow and I believe that it has found favor here and there. Even Suvorin, in *New Time,* praised it to the skies."[10] And also, "Perhaps I wrote it only a few days before my death? Not a happy thought. The void appalls me. Besides, I want to live! However . . . Come what may!"[11]

Despite the deterioration of his body, his literary pride was as tenacious as ever. With the doggedness of despair, he set about correcting the proofs of a new edition of his complete works. He wanted to leave a monument of faultless pages; if only he would be given time enough to complete this labor of perfection. "I am in a very curious position," he wrote to Tolstoy. "I am a healthy man who can neither stand nor walk nor move in any direction without experiencing unbearable pain, like the pain in a rotten tooth, in my left shoulder."[12]

In November 1882 he summoned all his strength to go back to Paris and spend the winter with the Viardots. In December the pain grew worse than before. His nightly dose of morphine was increased. He wrote to Annenkov, asking him to go through his papers after his death. Then, feeling a sudden surge of energy, he dragged himself to the rue de Rivoli on January 5, 1883, to watch the statesman Gambetta's funeral procession from the windows of some friends' home. "I have never seen anything to equal it and it is likely I never shall see anything to equal it hereafter,"[13] he wrote to Toporov. Among the mountains of flowers following the coffin, he was happy to see a crown of white lilac bearing the inscription, "To Gambetta, from the Russian friends of France." A week later, acting on the advice of his physicians, he had a neuroma "as large as an ugly plum" removed from his lower abdomen by a young surgeon named Paul Segond. In his condition, putting him to sleep was out of the question, so the extraction was performed without anesthesia. The operation lasted twelve minutes. A week later he wrote to Mrs. Polonsky, "The incision is almost completely healed, I had no fever at all, and in a week I shall be on my feet." But instead of improving after the operation, his general condition worsened with alarming rapidity. "My former complaint has returned with redoubled violence," he was soon telling Toporov. "I have never been in such pain. I can neither stand nor walk nor even lie down, and without the morphine injections I should not be able to sleep."[14] Now it was not just his left shoulder that pained him; his whole back and chest were pierced by furious stabs that left him gasping. Charcot came to examine him again and solemnly informed him that he was suffering from neuritis. Presumably out of charity, he was concealing from his patient the fact that he had cancer of the bone marrow. After Charcot's visit, the pain grew worse than ever. Poultices, chloral, chloroform—not even they could keep him from crying out. A few days later, however, an abscess of which he had been complaining for some time burst, releasing a flood of pus and blood, and brought so much relief that he wrote to Annenkov, "Maybe this time I am finally going to get well."[15]

Whenever his physical tortures relented for a moment, their place was taken by the anxiety his daughter was causing him. The poor woman had been forced to leave her husband and was hiding with her children, Jeanne and Georges-Albert, at the Hôtel de la Couronne at Solothurn in Switzerland. Turgenev sent her money regularly. On February 21/March 5, 1883 he wrote, in French, and in a shaky hand, "Dear Paulinette, Here are your four hundred francs for the month of March. My health is hardly better and I spend my days in bed. Kisses to you and your children."

Taking advantage of a slight improvement in his condition, Alphonse Daudet came to see him on the rue de Douai. "As always, the house was full of flowers," Daudet wrote. "As always, there were the light, clear voices at the bottom of the stairs and the friend above, on his couch: but so weak, so changed!" Turgenev talked about his ordeal as a true man of letters, for whom every slightest detail is significant. "Not having been given chloroform, he described the removal [of the cyst] with every detail perfectly clear in his memory," Daudet went on. "First, there was the circular sensation of a fruit being peeled, then the sharp pain of cutting into the flesh." In conclusion, Turgenev told Daudet, with his customary lack of affectation, "I was analyzing my sufferings so that I could tell you about them at one of our dinners, thinking you would be interested."[16]

In mid-April 1883 it was decided to take Turgenev back to

Bougival. He was carried downstairs in the servants' arms. On the lower landing Louis Viardot, also gravely ill, was waiting for him, gaunt and haggard in his wheelchair. The two old friends shook hands in silence and exchanged a long, desolate look. At last, they murmured "Adieu." They never saw each other again.

Louis Viardot died a few days later, on May 5, 1883, at the age of eighty-three, with his wife at his side. Having been a confirmed atheist all his life, he was buried with a civil ceremony only, in the Montmartre cemetery. A week after his funeral Pauline Viardot resumed her singing lessons. Then the whole family joined Turgenev in Bougival. The loss of Louis Viardot had so weighed him down that it seemed to have taken away his last ounce of energy. He felt that he had lost a friend of forty years' standing, a man with whom he had translated many books and shared countless days of shooting in the field, a man whose wife he had secretly coveted. What remained now of all those years of comradely conversation and ambiguous affection? It seemed to Turgenev that Louis Viardot, in dying, was showing him the way to go. "How I should like to join my friend now, without any more waiting!" he sighed. And he wrote to Mrs. Polonsky, "Far from abating, my illness is growing terribly strong. My suffering is constant and unendurable. Despite the fine weather I have lost all hope. The thirst for death is growing within me."[17] The pain was so excruciating at times that he begged Pauline Viardot to throw him out the window. At times, too, his mind was muddled by morphine. Sometimes he imagined he was being attacked by monsters at the bottom of the sea, sometimes he thought people were putting poison in his food. Pauline Viardot was nursing him patiently and competently; suddenly she appeared to him as a sort of Lady Macbeth. She had hired two professional nurses, a man and a woman. Turgenev accepted their presence with resignation, even gratitude. In a moment of lucidity he determined to write to Tolstoy, begging him to forget all his philosophical meanderings and return to literature. There was no jealousy in this man on the threshold of death, but a profound, total devotion to art. He took a pencil and scrap of paper and scribbled: "My good and dear Leo Nikolayevich, I have not written to you for a long time because I was and still am, to tell the truth, on my deathbed.[18] I cannot get well, it is pointless even to think it. I write you chiefly in order to tell you how happy I am to have been your contemporary and to make one last, sincere appeal to you. My friend, return to literature! That gift came to you from the same source as the rest. Oh, how happy I should be to think that this letter might have some influence on you!

I am done for, the doctors don't even know what name to give to my illness. Gouty stomach neuralgia! I can neither walk nor eat nor sleep. It bores me to talk about it. My friend, great writer of the Russian land, hear my prayer. Let me know you have received this scrap of paper, and allow me to embrace you one last time, hard, very hard, you, your wife, and all your family. I cannot go on, I am tired."[19] Tolstoy was touched by this appeal from a dying man, but did not feel that it was essential to reply. He was to reproach himself bitterly.

In June Turgenev's thoughts turned back to his youth, and he wanted to write the true story of the shipboard fire on his first trip to Germany, but he couldn't hold a pen or pencil, so he dictated the story in French to Pauline Viardot. A few weeks later he had another idea: a short story to be called "An End." This time Pauline Viardot took his dictation in a mixture of French, German, and Italian. The hero of "An End" is a young Russian nobleman of violent temper who has fallen upon hard times and dies murdered. Exhausted by his illness, hanging on by sheer will, Turgenev, in his retreat at Bougival, pored through his memory and let his thoughts carry him back to Russia. Maybe he would have been better off dying at Spasskoye instead of on this foreign soil where everybody around him spoke French. No, no, he could not have managed without Pauline. In herself, she filled the place of all he had lost when he left Russia. He told Stasulevich, who came to see him during a trip to France, "I should like to be buried in the Volkov cemetery [in St. Petersburg], near my friend Belinsky. Of course, I should like best of all to lie at the feet of my master Pushkin; but I don't deserve such honor."[20]

He knew now that his days were numbered; but perhaps it was better that way. He was sixty-five, and felt that he had lived too long and written too much. Immobilized in his big canopy bed, all he saw of the universe were the walls and furnishings of his bedroom. Waves of delirium followed in rapid succession. He complained constantly of being attacked by Assyrian soldiers, he tried to hurl stones wrenched from the ramparts of Nineveh at the people around him. On August 21/September 2, 1883 Prince Meshchersky came to Bougival and found the entire Viardot family assembled at the dying man's bedside: Pauline, her son Paul, her two daughters Claudie and Marianne, and her sons-in-law Duvernoy and Chamerot. All were anxiously watching the progress of disease and death on the emaciated face with its dream-drowned eyes. He was speaking Russian to these French people who couldn't understand him, reciting verses from his childhood. Suddenly he murmured, "Come here, closer, closer, let

me feel you beside me . . . The time has come to take my leave
. . . Like the Russian tsars . . . Tsar Alexis, Tsar Alexis . . ." For a
moment he seemed to recognize Pauline Viardot and was clearly
heard to say "This is the queen of the fairies! How much good she
has done!"

The women withdrew for the night, while Meshchersky, Paul
Viardot, Duvernoy, and Chamerot sat on at the sick man's bedside.
He had been given a large injection of morphine and swallowed a few
sips of milk. In the morning of August 22/September 3 he grew
restless again. His features worked, his breathing became irregular,
reddish spots broke out on his hands. Around two in the afternoon,
he tried to raise himself higher on his pillows, his brows knitted in a
painful grimace, a rattle issued from his sagging mouth. Then came
immobility, the mineral silence of death. The women burst into tears,
the men stared at the floor. Laid out for burial, Turgenev's features
reappeared in all their pacified comeliness. It was as if he had at last
solved the problem that had tormented him his whole life long—that
of belonging to two countries. "One might have thought he was about
to smile," Pauline Viardot wrote to Ludwig Pietsch. His friends sent
for a photographer and a caster to mold the death mask. They sent
telegrams all over Europe, beginning with Paulinette in Switzerland.
Pauline Viardot and her daughter Claudie, half blinded by tears, made
a number of drawings of Turgenev on his deathbed.*

The religious ceremony was held in Paris, in the Orthodox
church on the rue Daru. According to Edmond de Goncourt, it was
attended by "a whole little host of giant-sized persons, flat-featured
and bearded like God the Father, a whole little Russia whom no one
had any idea was living in the capital."[21] The body went to Russia by
train. At the Gare du Nord, Ernest Renan and Edmond About made
speeches.

Meanwhile, in Russia, the newspapers had received a secret circular from the Minister of the Interior, forbidding them to make public
the measures adopted to forestall any disturbance at the funeral—
because the news of Turgenev's death was felt in all Russian circles
to be an event of national importance. In dying, the man who had
been so derided during his lifetime left an impression of a void that
could not be filled. Confronted with his remains, the whole of society
discovered that it had a bad conscience because it had not attached

*The chalet at Bougival has recently been redecorated and converted into a Turgenev
museum. Pauline Viardot lived until 1918. Turgenev's daughter, Paulinette, was
widowed shortly after her father's death and died in 1919.

enough value to this stubborn, moderate, tenderhearted liberal who, in his lifetime, had combined a love for the people and a love of culture, faith in Russia, and admiration for the West. At last, the people who wept over his novels were united with those who respected his ideas; there was unanimity between left-wing intellectuals and delicate females, lovers of poetry and seekers after truth, artists and men of action. Turgenev was coming home triumphant, but too late to savor the irony of this final about-face in the attitudes to his career and his work. "I was expecting Turgenev's death," Tolstoy wrote to his friend Strakhov, "and yet I think of him very often."[22] And later, to his wife, "I keep thinking of Turgenev all the time, and I care about him terribly, and I pity him, and I reread him. I am living with him constantly . . . I have just reread 'Enough.' Read it, it's a marvel."[23]

As the days passed, the authorities grew more and more nervous. No author whose death creates such waves in public opinion can be anything but a troublemaker. The terrorists published a proclamation hailing him as the friend of all revolutionary youth. The political prisoners took up a collection to buy him a wreath. St. Petersburg gave him a grandiose welcome. On September 27/October 9, 1883, an immense crowd, carrying posters and banners and sheaves of flowers, followed him to the cemetery. Claudie and Marianne, who had come with their husbands, stumbled along behind the coffin, dazed with fatigue and grief. All along the way, the sidewalks were black with people. Every window was a box seat crammed full of spectators. "There has never been before and no doubt there will never be again such a funeral as this," the publicist Gaevsky wrote in his *Diary.* "One extraordinary thing was the absence of any official delegations; there was not a single military uniform, not one minister, not even one high official of any sort. Visibly, the administration was frightened. In addition to the police, there were five hundred Cossacks at the cemetery, and in the inner courts of the houses and in their barracks the troops were ready and in fighting dress. Turgenev was the most peaceable man on earth; could he ever have dreamed that he would become so greatly to be feared after his death?"

But in spite of the great crowd, there were no incidents. Turgenev was interred in the Volkov cemetery, as he had wished, and not far from Belinsky's tomb. Many speeches were made in front of the gaping grave flanked by hummocks of flowers. The sun shone coldly in a cloudless sky. Huddled together, the friends stared fascinated at the coffin at the bottom of the grave. They were all mourning Turgenev, all thinking of his strange destiny. In all his travels so far from Russia, he had never forgotten it, and now he had come back to the land of his childhood. To his compatriots what mattered now was not his life but his work. And his work, although partly written abroad, was all Russian in its sensitivity, its language, and its thought. That he could be such an inspired hymnist of his native land, and at the same time remain so responsive to the call of Europe, was little less than miraculous.

NOTES

1 SPASSKOYE

1. Yakov Patrovich Polonsky, *Turgenev at Home* (most likely a publication in Russian).
2. Ibid.
3. Letter, April 13, 1875.
4. *Journal* of the Goncourt brothers, January 27, 1878.
5. Ibid., March 2, 1872.
6. Turgenev, *Literary Reminiscences and Autobiographical Fragments*.
7. Ibid.
8. Letter, March 26, 1837.

2 STUDY AND ROMANCE

1. Turgenev, "Un incendie en mer" ["A Fire at Sea"], an autobiographical story dictated to Pauline Viardot in French, in 1883.
2. Letter, March 17, 1839.
3. Letter, November 13, 1838.
4. Ibid.
5. Letter to Turgenev, October 16, 1840.
6. Turgenev, *Literary Reminiscences and Autobiographical Fragments*.
7. Letter, July 4/16, 1840.
8. Letter, March 20, 1842.
9. Turgenev-Litovinov.
10. Letter, June 25, 1843.
11. Letter, June 19, 1843.
12. Letter, November 1843.

3 PAULINE VIARDOT

1. Letter from Herzen to Ketcher, March 11, 1844.
2. Turgenev, *Literary Reminiscences and Autobiographical Fragments*.
3. Belinsky, *Russian Literature in 1845* (most likely a publication in Russian).

4. Letter, March 31, 1843.
5. Jitova, *Reminiscences of the Turgenev Family.*
6. Letter (in French), November 8, 1846.
7. Letter, September 5/17, 1847.
8. Letter (in French), December 2/14, 1847.
9. Letter (in French) to Pauline Viardot, January 5/17, 1848.
10. Constantine Leontyev, *Turgenev in Moscow* (most likely a publication in Russian).
11. Letter (in French), January 5/17, 1848.
12. Turgenev, *The Man in Gray Glasses, Reminiscences of the Year 1848.*
13. Letter (in French), April 19/May 1, 1848.
14. Letter (in French) to Pauline Viardot, May 3/15, 1848.
15. Ibid.
16. Letter (in French) to Pauline Viardot, June 8/20, 1848.

4 MOTHER

1. Letter (in German), October 1/13, 1848.
2. Letter (in French), May 2/16, 1850.
3. Letter (in French), July 23/August 4, 1849.
4. Letter (in French), July 16/28, 1849.
5. Letter (in French), July 30/August 11, 1849.
6. Letter, July 11/23, 1849.
7. Letter (in French), July 17/29, 1849.
8. Letter (in French), May 4/16, 1850.
9. Letter, June 12/24, 1850.
10. Jitova, *Reminiscences of the Turgenev Family.*
11. Letter (in French), August 28/September 9, 1850.
12. Letter (in French), September 18/30, 1850.
13. Letter (in French), November 24/December 6, 1850.
14. Letter (in French), December 8/20, 1850.
15. Letter (in French), January 17/29, 1851.
16. Letter, November 1/13, 1850.
17. Ibid.
18. Turgenev, *Gogol, Reminiscences.*
19. Letter (in French), February 24/March 7, 1852.
20. Letter, February 26, 1852.
21. Letter to Turgenev, October 4, 1852.
22. Letter (in French), May 1/13, 1852.
23. Letter, September 14, 1852.
24. Letter, October 28, 1852.

5 AN ENDURABLE EXILE

1. Letter, October 17, 1852.
2. Letter (in French), October 13/25, 1852.
3. Letter (in French), April 17/29, 1853.
4. Letter (in French), May 12/24, 1853.
5. Letter, October 24, 1853.
6. Letter, November 25, 1853.
7. Letter, January 6, 1855.
8. Letter, November 1, 1854.
9. Nekrasov, "Comments on the press" (February 1856).
10. Letter, October 3, 1855, and from Henri Troyat's *Tolstoy* (New York: Harmony Books, 1980), 131.
11. This and all following material through "Without him, I am perishing of boredom" on page 53 is drawn from Troyat, *Tolstoy,* 132–39.
12. Fet, *Reminiscences.*
13. Told by Fet, according to Grigorovich, in *Reminiscences.*
14. Letter, February 8, 1856.
15. Letter, May 10, 1856.
16. Letter, May 9, 1856.
17. Letter, June 10, 1856.

6 PERCHED ON THE EDGE OF ANOTHER BIRD'S NEST

1. Letter, October 25/November 6, 1856.
2. Fet, *Reminiscences.*
3. Letter, September 18/30, 1856.
4. Letter, October 25/November 6, 1856.
5. Letter, September 13/25, 1856.
6. Letter, December 27, 1856/January 8, 1857.
7. Letter, November 25/December 7, 1856.
8. Letter, December 5/17, 1856.
9. Letter, December 8/20, 1856.
10. Letter, March 4/16, 1857.
11. Letter, February 17/March 1, 1856.
12. Henri Troyat, *Tolstoy* (New York: Harmony Books, 1980), 139.
13. Letter (in French), March 30/April 11, 1857.
14. This and the rest of the material in this paragraph is drawn from Troyat, *Tolstoy,* 173–74.
15. Letter, January 21/February 2, 1858.
16. Letter, March 27/April 8, 1858.
17. Letter, July 12/24, 1857.

18. Letter, July 13/25, 1857.
19. Letter, August 12/24, 1857.
20. Letter (in French), October 21/November 2, 1857.
21. Letter, October 31/November 12, 1857.
22. Letter, November 3/15, 1857.
23. Letter, December 22, 1857/January 3, 1858.
24. Tolstoy, *Diary,* September 4, 1858.
25. Letter, April 12, 1858.
26. Letter (in French), June 25/July 7, 1858.
27. Letter, April 7, 1859.

7 LIBERAL AND NIHILIST

1. Letter, mid-July, 1859.
2. Letter, February 18, 1860.
3. Letter, January 30, 1861, in H. Granjard, *Ivan Tourgueniev, la comtesse Lambert et "Nid de Seigneurs."*
4. Letter, February 16/28, 1861.
5. Letter to Turgenev, November 23, 1860, published by A. Zviguilsky in *Tourgueniev, Nouvelle correspondance inédite.*
6. Letter, February 25/March 9, 1861.
7. Letter, March 22/April 3, 1861.
8. Letter, May 21/June 2, 1861.
9. Letter, June 7/19, 1861.
10. This and all following material through ". . . I shall not open your letters any more than Turgenev's" on page 75 is drawn from Henri Troyat, *Tolstoy* (New York: Harmony Books, 1980), 219–223.
11. Fet tells the story in his *Reminiscences.*
12. Letter, May 27, 1861.
13. Letter, May 28, 1861.
14. Countess Tolstoy's *Diary.*
15. Letter, September 26/October 8, 1861.
16. Letter, January 24/February 5, 1862.
17. Turgenev, *Literary Reminiscences and Autobiographical Fragments.*
18. Turgenev, "About *Fathers and Sons.*"
19. Ibid.
20. Letter, April 14/26, 1862.

8 BADEN-BADEN

1. Letter to Herzen, September 26/October 8, 1862.
2. Letter to Longinin, September 26/October 8, 1862.
3. Letter, November 21/December 3, 1862.
4. Letter, September 23/October 5, 1862.

5. Letter, October 8/20, 1862.
6. Letter, January 22/February 3, 1863.
7. Letter, January 7/19, 1863.
8. Letter (in French), January 2/14, 1864.
9. Letter (in French), January 6/18, 1864.
10. Letter (in French), January 13/25, 1864.
11. *The Bell,* no. 177.
12. Letter, March 21/April 3, 1864.
13. Letter (in French), February 6/18, 1864.
14. Letter, March 26, 1864.
15. Letter (in French), January 19/31, 1864.
16. Letter (in French), January 24/February 5, 1864.
17. Letter (in French), March 3/15, 1864.
18. Letter, August 22/September 3, 1864.
19. Ibid.
20. Letter, January 26/February 7, 1865.
21. Letter to Borisov, March 16/28, 1865.
22. Letter to Borisov, September 30/October 12, 1866.
23. Letter, April 6/18, 1866.
24. Letter, April 12/24, 1866.
25. Letter (in French) to Pauline Viardot, March 22/April 3, 1867.

9 SMOKE

1. Letter, May 10/22, 1867.
2. Letter to Pisarev, May 23/June 4, 1867.
3. Letter to Herzen, May 23/June 4, 1867.
4. Letter, August 16/28, 1867.
5. Letter, December 27/January 8, 1868.
6. Letter, June 15/27, 1867.
7. Letter, June 28/July 10, 1867.
8. Letter, October 28/November 8, 1867.
9. Letter, July 26/August 7, 1867.
10. Letter to Borisov, June 16/28, 1867.
11. Letter, May 31/June 12, 1867.
12. Letter, June 16/28, 1867.
13. Letter (in French), June 17/29, 1868.
14. Letter, February 27/March 11, 1869.
15. Letter, June 5/17, 1870.
16. Letter to Annenkov, April 13/25, 1868.
17. Letter, January 10/22, 1870.
18. Ibid.
19. "Troppmann's Execution," June 1870.
20. Letter (in French), June 17/29, 1868.

21. Letter (in French), June 18/30, 1877.
22. Letter (in French), July 11/23, 1870.

10 WAR

1. Letter, July 15/27, 1870.
2. Letter, August 12/24, 1870.
3. Letter (in German), August 17/29, 1870.
4. Letter (in German), August 28/September 9, 1870.
5. Letter, October 16/28, 1870.
6. Letter (in French), November 23/December 5, 1870.
7. Letter (in French), November 10/22, 1870.
8. Letter (in French), February 15/27, 1871.
9. Letter (in French), April 24/May 6, 1871.
10. Letter (in French), June 1/13, 1871.
11. Letter (in French), August 17/29, 1871.

11 PARIS

1. *Journal* of the Goncourt brothers, May 5, 1876.
2. Ibid.
3. Alphonse Daudet, *Trente Ans de Paris.*
4. Letter, January 28, 1872.
5. *Journal,* March 2, 1872.
6. Daudet, *Trente Ans.*
7. *Journal,* May 5, 1876.
8. *Journal,* May 5, 1877.
9. *Journal,* March 5, 1872.
10. Daudet, *Trente Ans.*
11. Letter, September 17/29, 1876.
12. Letter, February 18/March 2, 1877.
13. Letter (in French).
14. Letter, February 5/17, 1872.
15. Letter, March 20/April 1, 1875.
16. Letter, April 6/18, 1874.
17. Letter, September 9/21, 1874.
18. Letter, January 15/27, 1877.
19. Letter, February 1/13, 1875.
20. Letter, October 5/17, 1875.
21. Letter, January 26/February 7, 1877.
22. Letter, February 8/20, 1877.

12 TURGENEV AND TOLSTOY

1. Letter (in French), June 6/18, 1876.
2. Letter, December 15/27, 1876.
3. Letter, April 18/30, 1878.
4. Letter, November 24/December 6, 1877.
5. Letter, June 29/July 11, 1877.
6. Letter, February 14/26, 1878.
7. Letter, April 17/29, 1878.
8. This and all following material through "I trust there will be, if not a smashing triumph, then a slow but sure conquest" on page 126 is drawn from Henri Troyat, *Tolstoy* (New York: Harmony Books, 1980), 404–409.
9. Letter, April 6/18, 1878.
10. Letter, May 8/20, 1878.
11. Letter, June 22/July 4, 1878.
12. P. Sergeyenko, *Tolstoï et ses contemporains.*
13. Letter, August 14/26, 1878.
14. Letter, September 30/October 12, 1878.
15. Letter, September 5/17, 1878.
16. Letter, September 5/17, 1878.
17. Letter, October, 1/13, 1878.
18. Letter, October 27/November 8, 1878.
19. Letter, November 15/27, 1878.
20. Letter, November 22/December 4, 1878.
21. Letter, December 28, 1879/January 9, 1880.
22. Letter, December 28, 1878/January 9, 1879.
23. Letter, November 25/December 7, 1875.
24. Letter (in French), January 9/21, 1879.

13 THE LION

1. Letter, February 20/March 4, 1879.
2. Letter, March 14/26, 1879.
3. Marya Savina, *Reminiscences.*
4. Letter, April 5/17, 1879.
5. Letter, June 12/24, 1879.
6. Letter, October 5/17, 1879.
7. Letter (in French), April 14/26, 1879.
8. Letter, August 27/September 8, 1879.
9. Letter, October 27/November 8, 1879.
10. Letter, October 31/November 12, 1879.
11. Letter (in French), October 25/November 6, 1879.

12. Letter, January 12/24, 1880.

13. Letter (in French), August 18/30, 1879.

14. *Journal* of the Goncourt brothers, February 1, 1880.

15. This and all following material through "... Turgenev repacked his bags and left, his mission a failure" on page 136 is drawn from Henri Troyat, *Tolstoy* (New York: Harmony Books, 1980), 417–18.

16. Sergey Tolstoy, *Sketches of the Past.*

17. Letter (in French), May 11/23, 1880.

18. Letter (in French), May 15/27, 1880.

19. Letter, April 24/May 6, 1880.

20. Letter, May 17/29, 1880.

21. Letter, May 19/31, 1880.

22. Letter, June 11/23, 1880.

14 PRESENTIMENTS

1. Alphonse Daudet, *Trente Ans de Paris.*

2. Letter, December 10/22, 1880.

3. Letter, January 26/February 7, 1881.

4. Letter, February 16/28, 1881.

5. Letter, February 15/27, 1881.

6. A. J. Lukanina, *Reminiscences.*

7. Letter, February 25/March 9, 1881.

8. Letter, March 6/18, 1881.

9. Letter, March 25/April 6, 1881.

10. Yakov Patrovich Polonsky, *Reminiscences.*

11. Letter, July 22/August 3, 1881.

12. Letter, August 10/22, 1881.

13. Letter, August 19/31, 1881.

14. This and all following material through "August 22. Turgenev—cancan. Sad." on page 148 is drawn from Henri Troyat, *Tolstoy* (New York: Harmony Books, 1980), 433–34.

15. Turgenev's words were reported by Sergey Tolstoy in *Sketches of the Past.*

16. Letter, September 23/October 5, 1881.

17. Letter, September 28/October 10, 1881.

18. Letter, October 18/30, 1881.

19. Letter, December 2/14, 1881.

20. Letter, March 13/25, 1882.

21. Letter (in French), February 14/26, 1882.

22. Letter, May 30/June 11, 1882.

23. Letter, April 11/23, 1882.

24. Letter (in German), April 24/May 6, 1882.

25. Letter, May 8/20, 1882.

26. Letter, May 18/30, 1882.

27. Letter, May 1/13, 1882, and from Troyat, *Tolstoy,* 452.
28. Letter, May 14/26, 1882.

15   HIS LAST RETURN

1. Letter (in German), July 18/30, 1882.
2. Letter, May 27/June 8, 1882.
3. Letter, October 22/November 3, 1882.
4. Letter, November 12/24, 1882.
5. Letter, May 30/June 11, 1882.
6. Letter, September 4/16, 1882.
7. Letter, June 1/13, 1882.
8. Letter, June 7/19, 1882.
9. Letter, July 27/August 8, 1882.
10. Turgenev, *Diary,* January 15/27, 1883.
11. Ibid., December 1882/January 1883.
12. Letter, October 19/31, 1882.
13. Letter, December 26/January 7, 1883.
14. Letter, January 17/29, 1883.
15. Letter, March 26/April 7, 1883.
16. Alphonse Daudet, *Trente Ans de Paris.*
17. Letter, May 12/24, 1883.
18. This and rest of material in this paragraph is drawn from Henri Troyat, *Tolstoy* (New York: Harmony Books, 1980), 452–53, 454.
19. Letter, June 29/July 11, 1883.
20. M. M. Stasulevich, *Reminiscences.*
21. *Journal* of the Goncourt brothers, September 7, 1883.
22. Letter, September 2, 1883.
23. Letter, September 30, 1883.

BIBLIOGRAPHY

TRANSLATIONS

TURGENEV, IVAN. *The Borzoi Turgenev.* Harry Stevens, trans. New York: Alfred A. Knopf, 1950.

———. *Fathers and Sons.* Rosemary Edmonds, trans. New York: Penguin Classics, 1965.

———. *On The Eve.* Gilbert Gardiner, trans. New York: Penguin Classics, 1950.

———. *Rudin.* Richard Freeborn, trans. New York: Penguin Classics, 1967.

———. *Sketches from a Hunter's Album.* Richard Freeborn, trans. New York: Penguin Classics, 1975.

———. *Spring Torrents.* Leonard Shapiro, trans. New York: Penguin Classics, 1980.

———. *Three Famous Plays.* Constance Garnett, trans. New York: Hill and Wang, 1959.

LETTERS

BEAUMONT, BARBARA, trans. *Flaubert and Turgenev: A Friendship in Letters.* London: Athlone Press, 1985.

KNOWLES, A. V., trans. *Turgenev's Letters.* London: Athlone Press, 1983.

LOWE, DAVID, trans. *Letters.* Ann Arbor, MI: Ardis, 1983.

STUDIES

BILLINGTON, JAMES. *Icon and the Axe: An Interpretive History of Russian Literature.* New York: Random House, 1970.

FENNELL, JOHN LISTER I. *Nineteenth Century Russian Literature.* Berkeley, CA: University of California Press, 1976.

FORD, FORD MADDOX. *Portraits from Life.* Westport, CT: Greenwood Press, 1974.

FREEBORN, RICHARD. *Turgenev: The Novelist's Novelist.* London: Oxford University Press, 1960.

GARNETT, EDWARD. *Turgenev.* London: W. Collins, 1917.

GRANJARD, HENRI. *Ivan Tourgueniev et Les Courants Politiques et Sociaux de son Temps.* Paris, France: Institute d'Etudes Slaves, 1954.

LEDKOWSKY, MARINA. *The Other Turgenev: From Romanticism to Symbolism.* Wurzburg, West Germany: JAL-Verlag, 1973.

LOWE, DAVID. *Turgenev's* Fathers and Sons. Ann Arbor, MI: Ardis, 1983.

NABOKOV, VLADIMIR V. *Lectures on Russian Literature.* San Diego, CA: Harcourt Brace Jovanovich, 1981.

PETERSON, DALE. *The Clement Vision: Poetic Realism in Turgenev and James.* Port Washington, NY: Kennikat Press, 1975.

PRITCHETT, V. S. *The Gentle Barbarian.* New York: Vintage Books, 1978.

RIPP, VICTOR. *Turgenev's Russia: From* Notes of a Hunter *to* Fathers and Sons. Ithaca, NY: Cornell University Press, 1980.

SCHAPIRO, LEONARD. *Turgenev: His Life and Times.* New York: Random House, 1979.

WORRALL, NICK. *Nikolai Gogol and Ivan Turgenev.* New York: Grove Press, 1982.

INDEX

Titles of works by Turgenev appear as subentries under the heading "Turgenev works." Turgenev's correspondence is indexed under the name of the recipient, e.g., Annenkov, IT correspondence with. (Turgenev's name appears abbreviated to IT throughout the index.)

INDEX

P112 :- PHANTOMS
THE DOG
KNOCK KNOCK KNOCK
THE WATCH
THE DREAM.
THE TALE OF FATHER ALEXEY
LIVING RELICS